Jewel Bridge

Early History of old Saratoga

Roger L Jewell

Published by Jewell Histories
Gettysburg, PA

First Edition
May 2018

1

To order contact:

Jewell Histories
143 Breckenridge Street
Gettysburg, PA 17325

jewellhistories@superpa.net

Phone 717 420 5344

Acknowledgments

I want to thank my wife, Mary E Jewell for her dedication towards the completion of this project. She not only edited the manuscript but also provided the interior sketches.

Mary also painted the cover art work. We called it "The Wedding Flower." It memorializes Jim and Betsey's wedding day, July 14th 1814 as indicated in the story. They stopped at Jewel Bridge on the way home to Jewel Corner.

I also want to thank my oldest brother Eugene Jewell for providing encouragement in recording the family records. He has expressed the solid family values that has been evident in the generations of the Jewell families. His leadership in the creation of the soldier's monument in our local (Brook Park Minnesota) cemetery, provides the recognition of the men who have had to put on the Nations Uniform in times of need. Like James Jewel in this story, most families can point to a beloved member who stepped forward. Through his efforts hundreds of people will remember their own family stories. To understand the hardships our forefathers suffered is to add meaning to each of our lives.

Introduction

During the early 1870s writers were getting ready for the one hundredth anniversary of the forming of the United States of America. Bobby O'Bryan, a New York reporter, was sent up to Saratoga Springs, one of New York City's resort towns. It was built next to the famous Saratoga Battlefield of the American Revolution. It was well known that large numbers of old soldier patriots had moved there after the war. It was Bobby's assignment to locate the families of some of these old soldiers and see what they had done after the war ended.

He meets ninety-six year old States Jewel, the son of a soldier killed during the war and the nephew of George Jewel, an old soldier who lived long after the war ended. The story is based upon the true story of States Jewel's family during the period from 1790 until the 1840s. It is also the story of my family. Harmon Jewel was my fourth great grandfather.

The main characters are all real people except Bobby. He is a composite of the author, Nathaniel B. Sylvester, who wrote *"The History of Saratoga County, New York"* and other people that were documenting this time of history.

States and his mother, Susannah, Uncle George and his wife, Hannah, all lived through the Revolutionary War. George's older children were born just before or during the war. George's younger children were born between 1788 and 1792 and were all raised in Saratoga County.

This story documents some of the early life of the county, from a time when Saratoga Springs had only three buildings up until the Jewels packed up their families and moved to Wisconsin in 1846. It highlights how the views and decisions of the founding fathers of the country affected this family and others around them.

There is considerable focus on George's son, James G. Jewel (Jim) as he and the family of his future wife are affected by the War of 1812. This was a war that was never understood by most and exemplified the early struggle to create a country out of thirteen separate colonies. Also, the problems of his son, Tom, and Harmon's

4

son, Joe, as they fought to end the feudalism of New York at that time.

Bobby's eyes are opened to the long battle the tenant farmers, like George and John, and their families suffered through before they finally abandoned the Hudson Valley Manors for true freedom in the west.

I hope the story will make clear the real process by which these United States of America were created, and also what needs to be done to maintain it as the free country it was intended to become.

Guide to the family members

Jewel Families
Will and Lizzy

George 1740 # and Hannah	*John 1746 and Elizabeth*	*Isaac (died 1783) Susannah*
Abraham (Abe) 1771	*Little Lizzy 1779*	*States 1777*
William (Will) 1773		*William 1778*
Danial (Dan) 1776		*Asa B. 1782*
Isaac 1780		
James George (Jim) 1788		
Hannah (Sissy) 1790		
Thomas (Tom) 1792		

George's Cousins

John Jr. 1740 #	*Harmon Sr. 1746 #*
Steven 1798	*Harmon 1770*
	Joe 1800
	George (Buddy) 1777

Three Revolutionary
Soldiers Saratoga #

5

Table of Contents

Chapter 1 - Bobby and the Old Man

Declaration of Independence, July 4, 1776

> *"We hold these truths to be self-evident, that all men are created equal, that they are endowed by their Creator with certain unalienable Rights, that among these are Life, Liberty and the pursuit of Happiness— That to secure these rights, Governments are instituted among Men, deriving their just powers from the consent of the governed, -- That whenever any Form of Government becomes destructive of these ends, it is the Right of the People to alter or to abolish it, and to institute new Government, laying its foundation on such principles and organizing its powers in such form, as to them shall seem most likely to affect their Safety and Happiness."* [1]

It has been nearly 100 years since July 4th 1776, when these famous words were put to paper. Men thought it time to celebrate their meaning.

Summer of 1873

As Bobby O'Bryan's train neared the Saratoga Springs station, he was going over his assignment. The boss back at the paper in New York City had said, "Get us a story on the soldiers of the Revolution. Everyone is working on the 100th reunion of the founding of the nation, let's see what kind of writer you are."

"Why me?" he thought. "All the hot stories in the south with the Civil War over and the political unrest, and my first story will be about the dust of history. Nevertheless, here he was and this was the story he must write. Where do you start to write a story about a bunch of dead people?

At least there was one good part to the job. Saratoga Springs was a pleasant place to spend a week or two. He could find a nice hotel and spend a few afternoons at the racetrack. He always loved to watch the horses run and this track was one of the best.

When he was checking in at the Clarendon Hotel next to the spring, Bobby asked the desk clerk where he might find some old people, someone who might be able to talk about the Revolutionary War. The young man looked around and then pointed to a frail old man sitting on the porch.

"That old man is States Jewel. People say he helped Mr. Holmes build the Old Columbian Hotel that burned a few years ago. Ever since he has been coming here, he doesn't like the new Union Hall and the masses of people around here all the time. The Columbian used to stand next to Congress Springs. States' wife, Clarisse, said that when she came to town there were only three houses in Saratoga Springs. Why not talk to him!" The clerk answered. [2]

Bobby walked up to the old man and stopped a respectable distance away. At first the old man didn't respond. After a few moments, the old man asked, "Are you looking for me? Speak up. I'm blind so I need to know where you are."

"Yes," Bobby replied, as he slid one of the chairs up to sit down. "I am looking for some of the older people who might have known some Revolutionary War soldiers. I work for the 'New York City Tribune' and my boss, Mr. Greeley, wants a story for the up-coming centennial."

"Well, you have come to the right man. As you can see I'm not too busy. I spend most of my time just sitting and enjoying my day here by the spring. I've been here a long time. My wife was even here when Congress Spring was discovered," [3] States went on. "What do you want to know about the soldiers?"

"I don't really know. I just need an interesting story. Who they were, what did they do, you know, that kind of stuff," the young reporter offered.

The old man fell silent for a moment with his eyes closed. "Great!" Bobby thought. "Now he will fall asleep on me, but it wasn't sleep that caused States to close his eyes. Being blind it didn't matter if they were closed or not, but when they were closed, he could see into the past as if he was right there.

"My father was killed in the war," States' voice almost seemed younger. "He was shot just a few days before it ended. My Uncle John, rode with Lt. Jacob Van Tassel, the man that Washington Irving wrote about in his short story, 'Wolfert's Roost.' In fact his daughter-in-law's family sold 'The Roost' to the Irving family."

"My Uncle George rode with Colonel Samuel Drake, also like my father. He fought in New York City, Peekskill and here at Saratoga. They were all part of the Westchester County Militia."[4]

"I thought the militia didn't really fight much. Most of what history says is that they ran when the fighting got hot," Bobby said.

He was surprised by a noise, as the old man's cane hit the porch deck. "Damn! Who told you that? Some wealthy manor lord's son, I would guess. The Westchester County Militia fought almost straight for eight long years.[5] If that's the rubbish you want to write about, then go talk to someone else." With that statement the old man shut up.

Bobby realized he had made a big mistake. This old man had the story he needed but now he just sat silently with a scowl on his face. If he was going to talk to this man he had better keep his opinions to himself and listen.

"I'm sorry, Mr. Jewel. I guess I had bad information," Bobby apologized.

States continued, "You sure did but it probably could be expected. Everyone was so bent on making George Washington a hero that they forgot who really won the war like the young men and boys that fought and died like my Pa." His scowl softened. That story has been told already anyway. My Uncle John kept a little story for our family.[6] You could stop and talk to my cousin down in Irvington and get it from him or you could just read Washington Irving's stories. You will probably get enough for a few lines." With this the old man leaned back in his rocker and pretended to go to sleep.

It was approaching noontime but it seemed like the interview was over. Bobby wondered how he could salvage the situation. It was apparent if he could get the old man to talk his story would probably differ from the dry old history he had read as a youngster. "I'll buy you lunch if you will give me another chance," he blurted out.

"Well that's better," the old man said as he appeared to come back to life. "After we get a good meal I will tell you about Uncle George and his cousin, John. They were soldiers, but the real story is what they did after the war. That story has never been told." With this the old man slowly rose from his rocker and started for the dining room.

"Maybe he is right. What about the old soldiers? What happened to them after the war ended?" Bobby jumped up and followed States into the dining room. "About his name, "States," he thought. "I will have to ask him about this."

After the meal, the two men returned to the porch. States smiled at the young reporter and said, "If I fall asleep you can just nudge me." They both laughed. The tension of the morning apparently was completely forgotten.

After seated comfortably, States began, "It was about 1790 when our life finally got back to some semblance of normal. My Grandfather Will had died in 1789, this was the same year that George Washington became our first President of the United States. My grandmother, 'Grandma Lizzy,' we all called her, died in 1790. I was thirteen years old that year . . . "I remember this is how it happened . . . . The day we left Fishkill . . .

Clarendon Hotel
"Leslie's Weekly" New York Public library[7]

Chapter 2 - Lizzy's Will, Aug. 3, 1790

In the name of God Amen, the third day of August in the year of our Lord, one thousand seven hundred and ninety and in the fourteenth year of American Independence, I Elizabeth Jewel, Relict and widow of William Jewel, deceased, of York Town, County of Westchester and State of New York, being infirmed in body, but in sound mind and memory, do make and ordain this my last will and testament in form following – that is to say, I give and Recommend my soul into the hands of Almighty God that gave it and my body I recommend to the Earth . .
.

Item: I give and bequeath to my beloved Son George Jewel and my beloved daughter Deborah, the wife of John Banker, the improvements of the farm now in my possession by virtue of a Deed of Gift to me, given by my Husband before his decease, to their proper use and to have forever. . . .

Item: I give and bequeath to my beloved Granddaughter Sarah Sarles the bed bolster and Pillows with the covering my brother Mathias Buckhout bought at his father's Vendue (public sale) forever.

Item: I give and bequeath to my beloved son, George Jewel, my clothes cupboard provided he buys one for my Daughter Deborah Banker. . . .

Likewise, I make constitute and appoint my beloved Son, George Jewel and my beloved Son, John Jewel my Executors . . .

In Witness whereof I have hereunto set my hand and seal the day and year above written,

Elizabeth Jewel signed . . .in the presence of each other, have hereunto subscribed our names, Abraham Buckhout, Mathias Buckhout, . . .

November 22, 1790

. . . The preceding is a true copy of (part) of the original Will of Elizabeth Jewel deceased and of the certificate of the proof thereof Philip Pell. [8]

Remembering 1790, the trip North to Saratoga

Young thirteen-year old States Jewel sat on the trunk of his mother, Susannah, which was tied on the bow of Captain Van Tassel's Sloop. His job was to watch his two younger brothers and 'see to it they didn't fall into the river.' States knew there was no chance of that. William was nine and Asa was eight. But the boat was about to set off and their mother just didn't want any of the boys to wonder off or get in the way in the excitement.

States older cousins were helping Aunt Hannah secure their family's large clothing cupboard. This was the last item to be put on board. Hannah's grandfather had built it and she was very determined that it should not be damaged.

"Tell us again about Lake Saratoga," Asa begged. States was the only one old enough to remember how their father had described it . . . .

States began, "'It's a beautiful lake,' our Pa had said. It was full of fish and we could catch them from a small boat. There is a lot of grass for the horses[9] and, of course, it's where the old Red- Coat, Johnnie Burgoyne, had surrendered. Pa said it would be a fine place for Ma to raise us boys" . . . .

A tear came to States' eye as he remembered his Ma's promise to take her boys there. For a while he actually thought he would be able to meet his father there. But it was only a short time before he realized his father was dead and the only place he would ever see him again would be in heaven.

States went on, "Uncle George says the land he bought is covered with big pine trees, and he and his cousin John will be selling lumber to Mr. Washburn, one of the men he will be working with.[10] The land is about ten miles north of town and John and Steven will be living there."

"Aunt Hannah and Ma will be living in a house near the bridge on Fishkill. It's just two or three miles west of Saratoga. We will get to collect tolls from anyone who wants to cross with a wagonload of lumber or grain. I don't know how much we will be able to keep, but it will be something."

States stopped his story there as the plank to the dock was being lifted. The younger boys ran over to their mother where everyone was waving goodbye to the families on the dock. He spotted his cousin, Little Lizzy and smiled at her. She caught his eye and smiled back, waving frantically. She had told him she might cry but he shouldn't be concerned. She was just one year younger than he was.

Because it had been hard for States' mother with his father's death in the war, Uncle John took him sometimes. He and Lizzy became good friends. A sadness came over him as the sloop slipped away from the shore. For a moment he thought he might cry also, but of course, he couldn't do that.

States' mother, Susannah, cried easily as she watched the Fishkill dock grow smaller. It was hard to leave John, Elizabeth and all her friends. Thank God for Hannah. Without her this would have been impossible. Her brood of strong young men was always there. "Can I help with that?" "Let men lift that". . . They were no longer boys but young men.

For Hannah it was different. Her husband, George, was already up at Saratoga. But for Susannah, Isaac's grave,[11] marked by the small bolder, must be left behind. It was some comfort that Will and Lizzy were laid out beside him. She knew she must move on. She was only thirty-eight and some had said was quite attractive. One of her friends said she might find herself a man up in the wilderness. The men were supposed to outnumber the women quite substantially. She hoped the change would make it easier. When Isaac was killed just at the end of the war, it seemed so cruel. It was hard for her to let go.

"Susannah, you and Hannah may be more comfortable down in the cabin for a while. The boys and I can manage up here on deck," Captain Van Tassel said.

"Thank you. I believe I will do that," she answered. As she glanced at Hannah she could see her deep in thought. No doubt she also was trying to say goodbye to the home she had known for over thirty years. Quietly she let her feet search out the few steps to the small room below deck. Hannah's younger children were already there. Their sparkling faces were just what she needed. Full of questions and excitement, they brushed away her darkening mood.

Chapter 3 - The Hudson River Road

"The sloop, as its name indicates, is of Dutch origin . . . In its simplest form, it is a vessel of one mast, carrying a mainsail, jib, and generally a topsail . . . . For steering the sloop a long tiller was used instead of the wheel which was not introduced until later."

"The Dutch settlers of New Netherlands, as well as the English and French, who soon merged with them, saw the advantages of the sloop rig for the commerce of the river and the Sound." [12]

"In 1803 the celebrated river we were navigating, though it had all the natural features it possesses today, was by no means the same picture of moving life . . . The journeys up and down the river were frequently a week in length" [13] *ref, "Sloops of the Hudson"*

William E. Verplanck and Moses W. Collyer, G. P. Putnam's Sons, New York and London, The Knickerbocker Press, 1908

States woke up early on the second day. He didn't want to miss any of the trip. They had left the sheer rock cliffs and hills behind and they could see a few cattle and farms along the Hudson. The river tide was going out and the early morning wind had not yet started. Only a few men were up. He climbed among the boxes in the bow of the ship. It would not be long before his younger brothers would also begin waking up. His older cousins, William, sixteen, and Daniel, fourteen, were already awake.[14] Like him, they were just sitting on the deck among the boxes wrapped up in their sleeping blankets and not yet ready to start a conversation.

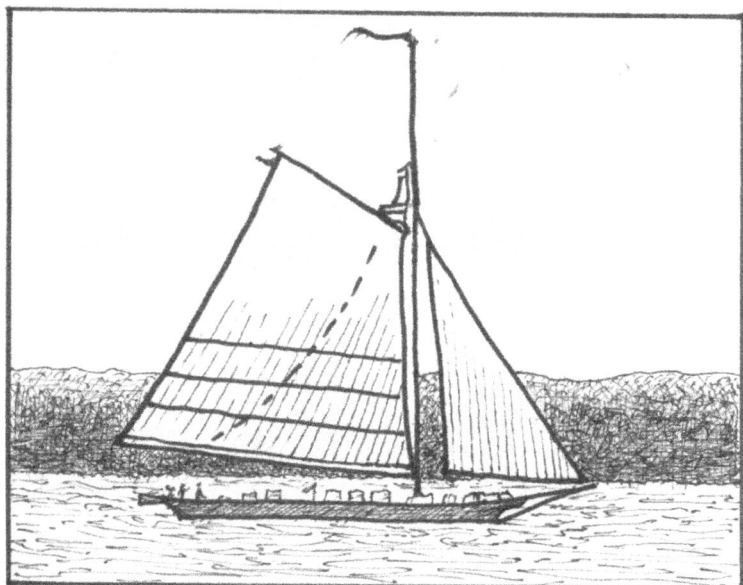

Hudson River Sloop
Sketch by Mary E. Jewell

When the talking did start it was Will that posed a question. "I wonder if the ghost of Jane McCrea is really walking around in our woods looking for her hair, like Uncle John said."[15]

Both Dan and States laughed. "I doubt it," Dan piped in, "You know how Uncle John likes to tell ghost stories. I think a wolf, bear or panther might be something to be more afraid of, but Pa says, 'even though they are big enough to really hurt you, they won't hurt you either, if you don't bother them.'"

"Your Pa sure knows a lot about the big pine woods," States broke in.

"He's been walking the woods looking for timber trees since he was about your age," Will answered.

States could hear the pride in his cousin's voice. "Grandpa Will took him in the woods when he was only twelve because he was the oldest," Will went on.

"I'm going to be a woods walker for some big mill," Dan added. "It would be more fun than pulling on a saw all day. Maybe I'll bring in the log rafts like we did sometimes on the Croton River with Pa."

"You can have that. I want to raise horses and go fishing in Saratoga Lake. Maybe I will have my own boat. People say that, in a small lake like Saratoga, a small boat is all you need," States explained.

States understood why Will and Dan were proud of their Pa. His Uncle George had fought in the War. He and Uncle John, like his own Pa, had ridden against the famous Cowboys in Westchester County. When he was young he rode rafts of floating logs down the Croton River. He and his brothers had helped build the bridge at the mouth of the Croton for Colonel Aaron Burr during the war. Even today he was building a bridge and house on Fish Creek in Saratoga.

"Yes," States thought, "Uncle George was a man that could do things and he was glad to have him for an uncle." His mother had often said that 'he had loved his younger brother, and your father, very much and promised your Pa as he was dying, he would keep an eye on you boys.' And that's what he was doing. That's why he and Hannah had taken them along to their new home in Saratoga.

18

States was not as sure of the big woods as Will and Dan. He didn't really want to see over the next mountain. He just wanted to have a nice field to raise horses. He loved to race the young colts and, even at this young age, he could recognize a good horse. In this way, his mother said that he took after his Uncle John.

As he thought of his Uncle in Tarrytown, he realized he would miss him. He wondered if his cousins could see the wetness that seemed to be forming in his eyes. He pretended to sleep as the breeze picked up a little. The crew was preparing to lift the sail and get under way. Will and Dan began helping the skipper, but since he wasn't needed he just sat quietly amongst the boxes, lost in deep thought. He was trying to understand the changes that were coming to the family. Uncle George had told him it was a new time in a new nation and everyone needed to be part of it. All of a sudden he felt small. At thirteen, was he ready? It was hard to be confident with having no father in a new and wild land. His mother called him her little man, but for just a moment he was not sure he wanted to be a man yet.

George Jewel stood on the log deck and looked out across Jesse Toll's Fish Creek Mill Pond. But his thoughts were about the old mill just below Pine's Bridge on the Croton River. As he waited for the last log to go through the saw, his mind drifted back . . . .

'It was time to move,' his father had said just a few months before he died: It was in the fall of 1789. Now he was here to bury his mother, Lizzy, and finalize her will, only a year later. [16]

He and cousin John at Fishkill had already made up their mind they would follow the logs. This time they could buy the land. When the logs were gone they would still have the farms. They knew some of the Mohawk Indian lands north of Saratoga Lake were available to buy. But Hannah had recommended that he take the offer from Stephen Van Rensselaer instead. 'You can't just drop our babies at the foot of a big white pine tree like a mother bear does with her cubs when she needs to hunt. They need a school and friends. Besides your skills are worth more than that of a common logger.'

George knew she was right, but he would not be able to buy the land along Fish Creek where the Van Rensselaer leased him the rights to build the bridge and house. The family had agreed to do both.

John, his son Stephen and George's oldest sons, William and Daniel, would work the small family mill on their own lands on Snook Creek. George would build the bridge on Burgoyne Road about two miles west of Schuylerville.[17] Ebenezer Ketchum, John's friend would help run their mill. The new bridge would allow them to bring wagon and sleigh loads of lumber from Jesse Toll's mill to the Hudson River at Saratoga. The small boys would be able to collect a few cents toll on each load of other goods that crossed it.

Everyone had agreed. The final plan had a much greater chance for success. The combination of both cash work and subsistence farming took away the risk of a simple job. The first task was the bridge, then the house. Stephen Van Rensselaer provided most of the bridge materials from the sawmill at Victory. George needed to buy his own lumber for the house. To get this he had agreed to work some for Jesse Toll at his new mill just two miles north of Jewel Bridge.

With the will completed, he and the two oldest boys left for the trip north. They were going to ride horses and take a work team on lead. The family mill and larger tools would be taken north when the family land purchase was final. The small woodworking tools were loaded on the workhorses backpack style. They would only need personal tools since Van Rensselaer had promised to supply the heavy tools needed to put up the bridge.

George would be working to supply logs for both General Schuyler's and Jesse Toll's mills,[18] a woods walker and log broker rolled into one. It provided the freedom he needed to produce and sell his own logs and lumber from the family farms at Jewel Corner.

He worked closely with Mr. Washburn[19] who had the timber contracts with the schooner captains that went into New York City, or even all the way to England. This way Jesse and the mill manager who worked for the General at his mill in Victory would know there was a market for the type of lumber they were producing.

Later as George stopped for a moment, he and some of his friends from the mill were putting new boards on the walls of his house. This was the day Hannah would be coming north. The older boys had gone to help bring the family up. He must keep pushing or the house would not be ready when she arrived.

His mind went back over his decision to move north. It seemed clear at the time but now he was not so sure. He was really starting over. This shell of a house would need hours of work even after Hannah arrived. His land up by Fort Edwards was just wild Indian land. [20]The beautiful big pine trees had mesmerized him. It was wonderful timber land, but as Hannah had argued, a dozen children need a home, food and a warm bed. For this reason he had signed on with Stephen Van Rensselaer and here he was building another home on land that didn't belong to him.[21] And most of his time would be spent finding timber for other men's mills.

Of course Hannah was right. At fifty-two years of age, his knowledge was of more value than his muscle. Jesse had said he needed him to help develop the timber in the large lot number twenty-eight in the Saratoga Patent. Also Stephen Van Rensselaer was going to open up his large lot number twenty-seven in the same patent.[22] That was the reason for Jewel Bridge. The road went straight west from the sloop harbor at Saratoga to Jewel Bridge, then west through Van Rensselaer's lot tapping several thousand acres of good timber and farm land. Everyone realized George knew everything there was to know about finding timber and getting it to the mill. He also knew how to build the dams and bridges necessary to get it there. He had to admit, if things went well, both Jesse and the manager at Victory had promised to pay a fair premium for the logs he brought in. He and his boys could raft logs with the best of them.

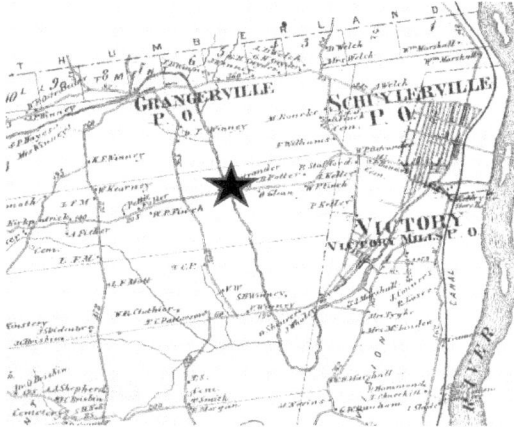

Jewel Bridge map location

As he pounded the nails into his new home he thought of his childhood on the Croton River. He and John used to skid the logs that his father had bought into the river. They would make up a small raft, tie the little skiff to it and ride the river to the mill. As they went under Pine's Bridge, they would loosen the boat and pull the logs to the eastern shore.[23] When they got to the mill Pa would throw them a rope and it would swing the raft into the stream outlet. George smiled to himself when he thought of those days.

But, as always, thinking of his home on the Croton River would bring him back to the war. Eight years of hard times. Up here he would miss John. William and Isaac hadn't made it through the war. Like so many, they paid the final price for freedom. That's what made this choice so hard. The war had granted freedom to some. George didn't begrudge his brother, John, the home farm,[24] but he understood he would have to make choices that would give his boys a better chance. Here he was, over fifty, and buying his first land. He was also aware of another thing. He really was not a farmer. He was a lumberman.

When he stood among the great white pine trees on the land that he and cousin John were buying, he felt it was almost a sin to cut them down. The Iroquois had protected that beautiful forest for hunting and trapping for so long that nothing really like it survived this far east.

Bobby asked "What about your Uncle George's cousin? I think his name was 'John.' What did he do when he got up here to Saratoga?". "I need to tie in the soldier part of his story."

"Don't get impatient, young man. I'm coming to that," States went on. "Well, back then we really didn't have a country yet. It was just a bunch of states."

"What do you mean?" Bobby injected.

"Well, you know before 1788 it was just a bunch of states all going their own way. You know the Constitution was not ratified until June 21, 1788 and George Washington didn't become the President until 1789. [25]That was the same year Grandpa Will Jewel died. When Grandma Lizzy died in 1790, for all practical purposes, there still was no national government. We had a President and Constitution but no one knew what it really meant yet. That's where the old soldiers had to step in and tell their congressmen what freedom meant. For example, in New York they had to protect themselves from having the wealthy taking over again."

"I don't understand what you mean, States?" Bobby stated.

"Well the treaty with England, for example. It said we were supposed to give the land all back to the Tories.[26] Instead the old soldiers had a better idea. Anyone who had raised arms against the Patriots was banned from our country for the rest of his life."

States stopped for a minute as if the young man needed time to understand. "That's what freedom meant. The old soldiers also now had the right to buy land. Before the Revolution only certain 'special' people could own land.

"What both George and John wanted to do was buy land of their own. John had been working on a lease from General Schuyler since 1784[27] and he wanted his own chunk of ground."

"Who was this John Jewel, your uncle's cousin? Tell me more about him," Bobby asked.

"We will have to go back a long way for you to understand what kept those two together," States continued. "In 1792, about two years after we had moved up here . . ."

Chapter 4 - The Children, 1792

Sleepy Hollow Church Records By: Yonkers Historical Library Association – 1901
1st Record Book of the Old Dutch Church of Sleepy Hollow 1st Reformed Ch. Of Tarrytown N.Y.
Jan Juel & Engeltie (wife), Johannis (son) Nov. 9th 1740
Staats Juel & Maritie (wife), Abraham – son, Nov. 9th 1740
Willem Juel & Elizabeth (wife), Jorus – son, Nov. 9th 1740 [28]

George sat quietly in the little wooden pew in the Sleepy Hollow Church. The toddler was asleep on his lap. As the sermon dragged on he let his mind wonder. This was the same pew his grandfather had sat in eighty-one years earlier. He liked the thought of the continuity. It was the same pew his father William had sat in fifty-two years ago, back in November 9, 1740.

Three babies had been christened on the same day. George wondered if he himself had fussed or had he just slept quietly like little Hannah was doing. It's funny how a day that you can't even remember can affect your life. It was his cousins, John and Abraham as well as himself that day. John Jr. and he were turned from cousins into brothers by the simple act of a joint christening. Maybe a similar strong bond would be created for his three children, James, Hannah and Thomas today.

First the joint christening, then riding together with Colonel Morris Graham at the battles of Saratoga.[29] Now John

26

Jr. and he were both taking their brother's families north, he with Isaac's boys and John with Harmon's boys. It seemed the families were stronger when they were bound together in God.

George glanced out the window on his left where he could make out the two brownstones that marked his mother and father's graves.[30] He had also been shown the sight where his grandfather was buried when he was little but, today when he looked, the old wooden marker was gone and he could no longer be sure where it was.

From where he sat he could not make out the simple granite bolder that marked Isaac's grave but he knew just where it was. He had put his father alongside him in 1789.[31] He liked to remember Isaac as he rode on his horse, Shadow, when he was eighteen, just before the war. He didn't know where William was buried. He had died in one of those stinking prison ships in New York City. It was only John and him now. When he put his mother next to his father in 1790 he knew it was time to move on.

General Washington had been President for about a year already and it was time for his cousin, John Jr., and he to get their own piece of land. That's why they were buying some of the Mohawk's pine timber lands up by Saratoga. It was just the right thing to do. He still was not sure if any of the promised grant lands would ever become reality. So he sold his land rights for silver with which he could buy a real mill site.

They didn't have a suitable church up there yet. Hannah had told George that they needed to get the children christened and that was that. When she said it in that stern no-nonsense voice of hers, he knew there was nothing left to do but arrange it. Hannah loved this little Dutch Church here on old Philipse Manor in Tarrytown. Her great grandfather was involved in building it when he ran the Grist Mill just across the road for the original lord of the Philipse Manor. When she was young she would often fish in the mill pond with her numerous cousins.

He knew she agreed to go north into the wilderness with him only because of the children. She knew he was a lumberman and must follow the trees. He would always be where the next trees needed to be cut and the next bridge or mill needed to be built. George looked at Hannah, sitting alongside of him, trying to keep little James quiet. The baby, Thomas, still lay sleeping in Elizabeth's arms. His brother, John, sat beside her at the end of the pew waiting to be named as the boy's godfather. Just then little Hannah, stirred, bringing him out of his daydream. The day was June 12, 1792 and George Jewel was about to christen his three children in the Sleepy Hollow Church. [32]

Sketch of, The Old Dutch Church)[33]

28

"But why here? Why did these families come to Saratoga?" Bobby asked.

States continued his story, "For that we need to go way back. John and his two younger brothers, Harmon and George, were all soldiers in the Revolutionary War. Both brothers also fought here at Saratoga as part of Colonel Graham's five-hundred, levie unit.[34]

"John and George, both born in the 1740s, made them the ideal age to be soldiers in 1775. There was quite a parcel of Jewel cousins in Fishkill in those years. Many of them were able to buy their own land in the 1740s and 50s so neither of John's brothers, Harmon or George, moved up to Jewel Corner. The only ones I got to know well were Harmon's two sons, George, and Harmon Jr, and later his grandson Joe.

"In the summer of 1777, the year I was born, the British had a plan to cut the rebellious states in half. Burgoyne was going to come south on the Hudson from Lake Champlain. Lieutenant Colonel Barry St. Leger, with about eighteen-hundred men, was going to come east from Fort Stanwix along the Mohawk River and meet him at Albany. The British General, Clinton, was supposed to come north and meet also at Albany, thereby holding the Hudson and cutting New England off from the rest of the colonies.

"The British needed to be stopped and it was up to General Schuyler with his Northern Army and New York's Governor Clinton with his militia. General Washington was tied up trying to defend Philadelphia. General Putnam was supposed to hold the Hudson River at the Highlands. The main problem being, there was not enough patriot militia to go around.

"At first Burgoyne moved south easily. Then Lieutenant Colonel St. Leger laid siege to Fort Stanwix with eighteen-hundred men. Governor Clinton called up one-thousand men of the militia. The Brave young Colonel Mellitus and the first five-hundred from Peekskill took the field first and moved to assist the defending of Fort Stanwix. They arrived about the time the siege began.

"Colonel Graham and Lieutenant Colonel Hopkin's five-hundred men from Dutchess County and farther south took the field in July of 1777.[35] They moved north to assist in the defense of the northern boundary also."

States ended his long explanation and became quiet. Bobby summarized, "That helps. So there were a lot of young Jewels and many of them became soldiers."

"That correct," States answered, "and not all were on the same side, but that's another story. . ."

As George sat on the intake wall of the mill he looked at the water of Fish Creek rolling over the dam. It took him back to 1777 when he also sat along this little creek, but that was during the second battle of Saratoga.

When the call went out for soldiers, George had temporarily moved his family north to Fishkill for their safety. Although he was technically part of the Westchester County Militia, they said it would be okay if he enlisted. They were all part of their local militias. So he joined with his cousins, John and Harmon, when they enlisted with Colonel Graham's *Levies* (500) men. They were not militia but were attached to the regular army enlistments which were from three to twelve months. George remembered well those hot marches. First they had traveled by boat to Albany, then by a

30

forced march west. Fort Stanwix was under siege and might fall any day. However, they had only marched one day west when they received the word that the British general had retreated and Stanwix would hold. He had been attached to the New York 3rd Regulars under General Benedict Arnold, a hard fighter. George knew several friends that had gone with him into Canada.

They were quickly turned around and brought back to Albany where they were assigned to the Northern Army under General Schuyler. They were a long way from being out of trouble. At Saratoga they were attached to General Glover's division.[36] This did not set well with General Arnold. He thought they should be kept with the New York contingent.

General Arnold had been very active in the first battle at Saratoga. He had even been seriously wounded. If George had been with Arnold he may lay dead on the field already. Many from the New York Regular Second and Fourth Regiments had died in those first furious days.

George and his cousins didn't mind being attached to Glover's Division. George had fought with him in 1776 at New York City. He knew he was a smart confident leader.

He could hear the small creek as it flowed past their position. It was only a couple miles from where they had started. They were watching the creek. If any of the British tried to get water they would fire. At night if they could not see, they would fire at the sound. The objective was clear, to keep up the pressure. He hadn't fired a shot in the two big battles, but at last they were getting some action. It felt good,

31

that he, John, and Harmon were doing their part to drive the British back to Canada.

The day Burgoyne surrendered was like none other in his life. They knew they had beaten one of the best armies in the world. Just a bunch of tenant farmers who were done being stepped on. They swore that day they would return and claim this little creek for their own.

John had gotten to the creek first. In 1784 he had already staked his claim to a small piece of leased land in Saratoga Village. Here it was, 1791, and George also had a piece of the little creek. Maybe someday Harmon or his boys could also lay claim to their own small part of this piece of history. It seemed strange to George how the war had changed him and made him part of itself.

That evening when he shut the mill door and walked the mile and a half down to Jewel Bridge, he felt content, secure in the fact that he had done his part. This United States of America would be a fine country in spite of the greedy. The land was big enough for everyone and more.

"So both men fought the British right here on Fish Creek and that is why they came back?" Bobby asked.

"Yes," States said. "Two came back. It was up to Harmon's sons if they were to take their father's place. Like George always said, 'war changes men.' It makes them want different things. "

"So that's why George and his cousin, John, were so close. They were christened together and fought together here at Saratoga," Bobby replied.

"Yes," States answered, "it formed a bond that was never broken."

"Did your mother find a new husband in Saratoga, States?" Bobby continued. He needed to thicken his story. He knew by this time Susannah had been deeply involved in the war as a soldier's wife in the area called the disputed lands of Westchester County. He wanted to know what part she played in the lives of these old soldiers.

"Well yes, she did, and it didn't take very long," States answered. "His name was Ebenezer Ketchum and he worked his good friend, John Jr."

Jewel Corner
Saratoga County East Map[37]

Chapter 5 - When Eben Met Susannah

Ebenezer Ketchum II, born January 26, 1752 in Wilton (Old Norwalk), Fairfield County, CT. Nathaniel Ketchum's Will ". . . my well beloved son EBENEZER KETCHUM, (Ebenezer's II father) all my land at Hoyts Plain and my swamp nearby it and one third of my comonage and the land becoming due upon the same. Also my weaving loom and tackling." [38]

"Yes, Bobby, Ebenezer Ketchum became my stepfather," States began. "Everyone called him, 'Eben.' He was part of the Nathanial Ketchum clan. They had all come from Wilton in Fairfield County, Connecticut. He was born there on January 26, 1752. His father, also Ebenezer, and his two brothers, Elihu and Joseph, had all moved west about then, first into the area of New Canaan, Connecticut, then on into Dutchess County, New York. By the time the war started in 1775, his family lived along the Green River at Austerlitz. He first met my mother through George's cousin, John. They were good friends. They both worked for General Schuyler in his mills. He used to tell me how she affected him right off. Today you might say 'love at first sight.'"

Eben sat at a little table in the corner of the large room. He and it were covered with sawdust. The groaning of the blade moving up and down lulled him into daydreaming and going over his life and thinking about the young woman he had just met. She was the same age as he was, thirty-eight. In 1775 Susannah had lived along the Croton River on Cortlandt Manor.

She must have been married about then, because her oldest boy was born in 1777.[39]

He remembered the summer of '77' well. It was then that Burgoyne's Indians scalped the McCrea woman. Everyone had been so angry, that when General Washington called for the militia, he and his brothers, Stephen and John, all signed up. That was when he first saw the mills at Saratoga. First, the battle for Fort Stanwix and then the two big battles here on these Saratoga fields. As boys they were so proud when the Redcoats stacked their arms at the old fort over by the river and were marched away. Many of them signed up right then in the New York Regulars. The rest of the war was just a mess in his mind. Eben didn't think of it much anymore.

How had the years gone so quickly? Susannah had raised three boys and he had just returned home in '83.' It had taken him seven years to get where he was now, making flour, cloth or lumber, always in a mill somewhere. The war had affected him at it did everyone. But she had snapped him out of it. This beautiful young woman had been hurt by the war also. The last seven years she had struggled to let go of her husband's death. He thought, "What was his name? Isaac. Yes, Isaac! George Jewel's younger brother."

After raising three little boys by herself, Susannah also might be ready to start life anew. The country had a new President and he had just ordered a national census. Yes, 1790 was the time for new beginnings. Maybe he could marry this woman and start his own family. He was still young and so was she.

Just then the sawmill log came to the end of the board. The changing noise let him know. One of his helpers spoke louder above the machine noise, "Eben! Where do you want me to put these boards?" He looked up, momentarily confused. Then he answered the man and got back to work . . .

"So Susannah met a man who worked in a sawmill?" Bobby asked.

"Yes, right away. It was General Schuyler's sawmill at Victory on Fish Creek. They were married within months and quickly started giving me little half-sisters and a brother."

"He didn't work at Jess Toll's Mill then?" Bobby asked.

"No, at first he worked for General Schuyler's linen mill but the dust affected him and he changed over to the sawmill. Then when Eben married my mother, they moved up to Jewel Corner and worked at the the family mill. He and John had shared a one-hundred and twenty acre farm and were friends before my family came north. When George finally got the family mill going, he worked there. Eben had a lot of experience with all kinds of milling. Grist mills, linen mills and finally sawmills. Up until about 1800, when he died, we lived mostly at Jewel Corner."

"The Fish Creek operations were much bigger than our little mill. The General Schuyler mill at Victory and Toll's mill, in what is now called Grangerville, moved shiploads of lumber to New York and Europe."

"But, it's getting late. I better stop here. If you would like we could talk again tomorrow."

The old man prepared to leave as Bobby gave his last comment, "Can we talk more about the old soldiers tomorrow and what they did with their lives?" The young reporter was not sure yet if he was getting anything he could write about.

"Sure!" States answered. "We could talk about how their sawmills helped to build New York and the ships in her harbors. Or didn't I tell you the Jewel families were long involved in building boats and ships. George worked on the ships that won the War of 1812. I'll see you for lunch tomorrow about noon then." And with that the old man shuffled away.

As Bobby sat there he glanced at his pitiful and scanty notes that he had written. He wondered, "Where was the story? These old soldiers came north and built some sawmills. So what? Hundreds of old soldiers built sawmills. But what was this? There was no nation then."

"And what was it like when the Constitution was being created? Did that one old soldier, Colonel Aaron Burr, the Vice President, actually shoot and kill another old soldier, Alexander Hamilton, the Secretary of the Treasury? Did Burr really think Hamilton wanted to bring back the king and the feudal system? No! He must have been joking. Alexander Hamilton was a hero, wasn't he? Maybe? Why did it take twelve years before the old soldiers were given the bounty lands promised eighteen years earlier? Why were the Revolutionary War pensions not granted until 1832, forty nine years after the peace was signed? Why should an old soldier wait forty-nine years before he received a pension?'

Maybe he was right. There was no country until the old soldiers fought with the wealthy and forced them to understand what it meant to be free men. Was the country still not completely functioning in 1812? Was that why the British with a few men walked in and burned Washington? This old man was there and that's about what he was saying. If that was true, it did take a long time to decide what freedom meant. And maybe States' Uncle George, and thousands of men like him really did have to create a new country, long after the hard fought battles of the war were over.

Chapter 6 - Military Land Grants 1790

John Buckhout - b. Aug 1758 Granted Lot # 96, in Township 20 Solon in Military Tract containing 600 acres . . . Lot was granted by letters of patent under the Great Seal on the State of New York, bearing the date 13, September, 1790. Land was bought by Paul Cornel in about 1811 or 1812 for $100. (Ref: New York Balloting Book, p – 112).

Bemard vs Germand. He provided a promissory note to John Buckhout of Fishkill, Dutchess County, in the sum of $200, dated Dec. 23, 1807 in exchange for conveyance of lot 96 in Solon (Present Day Cortland Co.) Onondaga County, that had previously been granted to John for his military service in the Revolutionary War. [40]

Note - John was Hannah's nephew and was raised on the same farm in Irvington with George's brother, John Jewel. It appears John Buckhout sold his 600 acre grant for 17 cents an acre.

After a good meal the old man sat down and was again ready to tell his story. "You wanted to know about what these old soldiers did. Was that it?" States asked.

"Yes, you said there was no nation then. What did you mean by that?" Bobby was trying to catch the thread of the story that he was alerted to the day before. "How did this affect George and the other old soldiers?"

"When we moved here in 1790," States began, "Our lives back then were primarily controlled by the State of New York.

The Governor and our State Assembly still wrote all the rules that affected our daily lives. People like Robert Livingston and John Jay had written the State Constitution in 1777. It was changed very little from the original Colonial Charter (The Charter of Liberties and Privileges' of 1683 and revised in 1691).[41] It still maintained the British structure which assured the culture class structure would survive. In other words, the governor and his council remained the supreme authority and, through the ability to appoint the judges and sheriffs, they maintained their power. Only wealthy landholders had a say in who was put on the council. After the war Alexander Hamilton married General Schuyler's daughter and became an important member of this New York ruling class.

"New England had the Massachusetts Charter which assured the rights of the town form of Government at the most basic level. This was designed to protect their manufacturing and shipping industries.

"Virginia had their Colonial Charter which assured the continuation of the large plantation owner class and still authorized slavery. Other states in the area, north and south, followed these general outlines. Pennsylvania was at first more like the southern model, but William Penn, after he found the Lord, had introduced changes early on that honored the small agrarian farmer to a greater extent.

"But poor people and non-landholders of New York still had no right to vote on the judges or sheriffs who ruled them.

"The effort to soften the differences between what was essentially three or four little countries were what the Constitutional Convention in 1787 and 1788 was all about.[42] The Congress of these 'United States' realized no real country had yet been established. The three basic elements of governance that they all agreed they needed at the federal level, were these: common defense, a national currency, regulation of international trade and interstate trade. It was also recognized that this national government would need to collect tax revenues to do all these things. All other elements of governance were jealously guarded by the states.

"The creation of the United States Constitution did not solve those differences, except on paper. The New York Governor, George Clinton, and men like him, were against the Constitution. [43]It would, when fully operational, severely weaken the New York State government system, especially the land-based aristocratic system they had worked so hard to keep in place."

"Wait! This is starting to sound like a history lesson. How did it affect old soldiers like George and John?" Bobby said.

"Well, I'm getting to that. The grant lands and pensions they were promised had to come from the Congress or our new President, George Washington. It was here in about 1790 that the first real effects began to be noticed. Like I said, Hamilton and the other rich Federalists were trying to reverse the power that the new Constitution gave to the common man. We all saw this as a betrayal. Officers, like General Phillip Van Cortlandt and Aaron Burr, stepped up and pushed Congress into action. Remember, there was no Saratoga County in 1790. We were still part of Albany County. Finally in 1792, New York State paid off the Soldiers Damage Claims and started making the Indian lands available for sale.[44] The national laws surrounding the Bounty Land Grants also started to move."

"So what you are saying is the national government was so weak that the states still were basically running the country," Bobby responded.

"Yes, and in New York it was not clear what the new country would look like when it was all over," States answered. "Saratoga was, of course, still run by Stephen Van Rensselaer, Alexander Hamilton and his father-in-law, Old General

Schuyler, all strong Federalists. A few miles north at Palmer Town were Indian lands of the Kayaderossera Patent.[45] They were surveyed and available through the thirteen patentees. Many of the officers and soldiers like George and John Jr were buying land in the area. Most of them were Jeffersonians.

"The political divisions were starting to be noticed in the state government. The people who rented from Van Rensselaer were not qualified to vote since they officially were not landholders. [46]While people with title to their property on the military tracts and, to some extent, the Kayaderossera patent did have a vote on New York's Upper House."

Chapter 7 - Hamilton's Land Policy 1790

"Hamilton offered a more detailed plan,"
"One, the facility of Advantageous sales, according to the probable course of purchases; the other, the accommodation of individuals now inhabiting the western country or who may hereafter emigrate thither." The first preposition was important to Hamilton."

"The less well-to-do persons were treated off handedly, . . . Hamilton, having satisfied himself that those interested in large tracts were of greater potential financial strength to the United States, stated that the general plan for the disposal of public land should have been predicated to their benefit."

The result was predictable. Large tracts 10 miles square were to be auctioned off in the large eastern cities. The very same lands people were already settling on the frontier. [47]

States opened the discussion with the following, "People in Saratoga County were not confused by the big words and flowery rhetoric of Alexander Hamilton. People realized his primary objective in land policy was to put the land in the hands of the wealthy speculators and manor lords, while at the same time making it impossible for the common ex-soldier to secure his own farm, forcing him to work in the eastern factories and rent from large manor lords."

"Luckily more rational heads held sway and property started becoming available to the common man out west. Sale sizes of public lands were reduced to one-hundred and sixty acres by 1803."

"However," States went on, "this did not affect the properties already patented in New York and it had no bearing at all to Stephen Van Rensselaer's extensive holdings."

"So what happened to your cousins, Daniel and William?" Bobby interrupted.

"Well, by 1797 they were both married. Daniel married a girl he grew up with in Yorktown and moved back down there. William married a young girl named Sarah and they ran Uncle George's mill at Jewel Corner. That's what everyone called our little settlement and mill on a tributary of Snook creek, near Gansevoort."

States went on, "Sometimes to support our new families we worked a while on the new hotels at Saratoga Springs as carpenters.

"With Dan's marriage, in 1797, and Isaac's coming of age, John Jr.'s nephews, Harmon and George, came north to Jewel Corner.[48] These were the sons of John Jr's brother, Harmon, of Fishkill, in Dutchess County. John Jr. had always maintained a close connection with his two brothers in Fishkill.

"My Uncle George also started looking for new opportunities for these young family members. Stephen Van Rensselaer was, at the time, offering what appeared to be a good deal for a poor man with a strong back.

"In 1800 George was a foreman during the construction of the bridge that Mr. Washburn was building across the Sacandaga River, near a community called Fish House.[49]

"Van Rensselaer was offering one-hundred and twenty acre farms on the other side of the river. They were free for seven years and then only a small rent per year after that. The Jewel family took one along the river. They called it the "Free Farm." It had a waterpower site and some good bottomland field."[50]

States continued his story, "When Harmon arrived in Jewel Corner he was single, but he soon met James Brisbin's daughter. They married and had a son named James Brisbin Jewel in 1797. Soon after he had a second son, Joseph H Jewel in 1800. They settled on the Free Farm about 1800 or 1801.

"James Brisbin was one of the first settlers in the area of Fort George. Some say the Brisbins knew well the McCrea girl that was scalped.

"At about the same time, Jim and Tom Jewel lived the carefree life of boys in the wilderness. If they were not fishing under Jewel Bridge, they were talking to travelers going up to see the spring. They would sell the travelers apples, fish or anything else that would bring a penny.

"Hannah realized little boys were best left to their own entertainment as long as they did their chores and collected the bridge tolls. She also noticed when little James, the most forward, stepped up in front of the big horses, put up his hand or wooden sword and said, 'that will be two cents, please.' Most of the drivers would smile and flip him the coins.

"Ma and we children had moved down to Saratoga Lake and bought our farms there in 1800,"[51] States added, as he wrapped up the summary, handed Bobbly some old family papers and shuffled home.

Chapter 8 - The Letter

Jefferson is Elected President: March 4, 1801 – March 4, 1809, Vice Presidents were Aaron Burr and George Clinton.

"If a nation expects to be ignorant and free, in a state of civilization, it expects what never was and never will be." Thomas Jefferson

When talking about a law he proposed to the Virginia State legislator: Jefferson also writes, that "of all the views of this law, none is more important, none more legitimate, than that of rendering the people safe, as they are the ultimate, guardians of their own liberty. For this purpose the reading in the first stage, where they will receive their whole education, is proposed, as has been said, to be chiefly historical. History by apprising them of the past will enable them to judge the future; it will avail them of the experience of other times and other nations; it will qualify them as judges of the actions and designs of men; it will enable them to know ambition under every disguise it may assume; and knowing it, to defeat its views." [52]

Ref. Thomas Jefferson's only significant book, *"Notes on the State of Virginia"* first published in 1785.

The neighborhood boy rode into the yard and jumped off his horse. Hannah noticed he was quite excited when he came to the door.

"Mrs. Jewel, the postmaster said that I should tell you that you have a letter at the post office!" the boy exclaimed.

"Young man, slow down! What are you saying about a letter?" Hannah asked.

"The postmaster says you have a letter over in the village," the boy continued. "Who do you suppose would write to someone here at Jewel Bridge?"

Hannah smiled, "Well, my brother, Captain Buck, can write," she said as if they received mail every day. But inside she also was getting excited and worried at the same time. It had been years since she had received a letter from Buck. She was not sure she would be able to decipher the cursive hand writing anymore. The only thing she ever read these days was the Bible and even that with difficulty. Since George could not read, the only news he brought home was verbal. A letter, now that must be something important.

"I saw it," the boy went on. "It was a folded piece of paper with a red piece of wax sticking it shut. The letter had some writing on the outside and the postmaster said that your names were written on it."

"Thank you for the message, Sammy. You can go now," she said as she noticed the boy still standing in front of her.

"A letter," he was mumbling as he climbed back on his little horse and rode off. He knew Mr. Jewel was quite important at the mill and that he had built Jewel Bridge. "But a letter," he thought. "Only the bigwigs got letters."

Hannah could hardly wait until that evening when George came home from the mill. "You have a chore yet to do this evening," she chided with a big smile on her face.

"What's that?" he replied. "I had a hard day at the mill."

"You will have to ride over to the village and pick up your letter," she laughed. "I won't be able to sleep a wink if I have to wait until tomorrow."

"A letter, no! Who would write us a letter? Who do we know that can write?" George wondered.

"Well my brother, Buck, for one," she said indignantly. "He knows I can read."

"Yes, the Bible. I can read the Bible too. John 3:16 . . . for God so loved the world . . ." Then he broke out laughing.

Hannah became serious. "I can read most of the words. It's only the big ones I have not heard that are hard." For a moment she was almost insulted. Then she laughed too when she realized he was teasing her.

"After supper I will ride into Saratoga and pick it up," George replied as he washed up for their evening meal.

It seemed like hours had passed when George finally got back from the village. It would soon be dark and Hannah was anxious to open the letter. The little children were all gathered around. Just for a moment again she became worried. What if something terrible had happened to someone in her family? She could see George was also worried. He could think of any good reason why anyone would write them a letter. Neither John nor Elizabeth could write. He took out his pocket knife and slowly pried off the wax seal and handed the single sheet of paper to Hannah.

"What does it say?" little Jim asked before she even had a chance to look at the carefully formed words.

Hannah knew right away the letter was not from her brother Buck. The two she had received from him were kept carefully with her special things. He didn't form his letters this neatly.

"Read it, momma!" the children shouted.

"Well, be quiet so I can," she answered.

It was hard at first, but soon the memory of her childhood studies started coming back.

"It's from your cousin, Little Lizzy, your Uncle John's daughter. She is a young woman now," Hannah explained. [53]

47

Dear Aunt Hannah and Uncle George and Family,

I hope this letter finds you all well. Martha Ferris's mother is teaching us how to read and write. Pa says, if you know how to make words, why don't you write Uncle George a letter and I will post it up to him. So I decided to do it. I may be spelling some of the words wrong but it's how they sound to me. Pa says Mr. Jefferson says we all need to learn how to read so the bigwigs can't cheat us so easy. Captain Ferris, Captain Dutcher and Pa are going to build a school by the creek. Pa says they can put it on our land up on the Albany Post Road. Pa says, what good is a post road unless you post something once in a while. Ha! I am being courted by John Storm. If we get married, our children could go to school on our own farm. I think it is very nice that Mrs. Ferris is teaching John and me how to read and write. Pa says it's because Martha, Mrs. Ferris's daughter, is sweet on our John, and Captain Ferris doesn't want to have to deal with another dumb Jewel. Ha! We are all well. I hope you can come on a visit soon. Remember, we have a very big house.

Love, Little Lizzy,, Ma, Pa, and John. June 21, 1797.

Tears came to Hannah's eyes. All of a sudden she missed that big house, John, Elizabeth, Little Lizzy and young John. She would always be Little Lizzy even if she was eighteen years old. The house that Grandpa George Jewel and his boys had built back in 1740 was a beautiful wooden home. The Jewels always built with wood. Of course, there was the beautiful stone fireplace in the corner of the living room. Hannah was brought back to the present by the children.

"Read more!" they were shouting, "Read More!"

"That is all there is," Hannah answered.

"Please read it again," George requested. "It makes me feel a little like I am there."

She could see the glistening of tears in her husband's eyes. He also had given up his home to move up into this wilderness. Sometimes she hated that decision but there had been no alternative. A lumberman must follow the trees. But this simple letter had brought it all back. The simple words on a single sheet of paper were as if Little Lizzy had reached over the miles and given her a kiss.

She remembered her youth on the manor. There had been no school up at Pines Bridge. Her mother had given her what little schooling she had received. It was much as Mr. Jefferson had said, "The Federalists, like Alexander Hamilton, were against teaching the children of the tenants. Otherwise, who would work in the factories or on the lord's farms?"

How could you cheat a man who could read the law or the contracts which they once had to put their 'x's' on? At that moment, something changed in Hannah. They would have a school also. It wasn't too late for her younger children.

As she reread the simple letter she promised herself she would find time to read. She would find papers and books to read to her children. As soon as possible she would talk with

Susannah. Eben could read. Most of the Connecticut men found ways to educate their children. The Jewels would start now.

"Isn't this a nice letter?" she found herself saying to the children. "Don't you think we should have a school also?"

"Yes!" the little ones all shouted gleefully together, But the older boys were not so sure. She noticed George looking at her in a strange way. Maybe he had noticed the change that had come over her. Or maybe he also realized that Mr. Jefferson was right. They would not be free of lords and kings until they could read the laws for themselves, even for the simple pleasure of communicating by letter with family and friends. Why should only the wealthy have that privilege? This letter, this one letter, had lit a fire in her heart. A fire that was to burn in the hearts of many, as common people realized they must school their children. No one any longer had the right to reserve education for only the wealthy.

Hannah, Susannah and several of their friends soon were talking of a school. It was not long before they heard from the landowners. "I will pay no tax on my land for a school to teach a bunch of young roughs. Education is something you pay for yourself." At first it looked like the idea would go nowhere, but the new government was considering new ideas. The Jeffersonian democrats were talking openly about public schools. Schools, where anyone could learn to read and write.

George knew when Hannah made up her mind it was useless to object. Besides, he thought she was right. The crooked leases being re-negotiated by Stephen Rensselaer and Alexander Hamilton were not abstract ideas. They would soon be coming up on the Free Farm. Harmon and Isaac were worried that they would have no right to run the mill when the water rights would be separated on the new lease. Little Lizzy had written it in the letter. You will need to learn how to read and write if you don't want to be cheated by the bigwigs.

When George approached Jesse Toll he knew where Jesse would stand. He owned all the land. Why should he want a school? George decided not to ask. Instead, he just told Jesse that he and some of his friends were going to put up a little building on the corner of his leased land where his children and a few of the neighbors could learn to read. The apparent harmlessness of the statement should not create a problem. Up in Palmer Town the Connecticut men had one and down in the village they had one. They would need to saw a few logs some Sunday afternoon for the lumber. The local men would donate the lumber.

"Who will teach the children in this school? And who will buy the books and slates?" Mr. Toll asked.

"We will find someone," George went on as if it had already been decided.

"I suppose it will be okay if you build it on your lot and the men donate the time and lumber. Maybe you could teach a few of these boys to count beyond ten," Jesse laughed.

"Oh, I think we could do that alright," George went on. "We might not need to hire Mr. Schuyler's engineer so often if a few of our own boys knew their numbers."

Jesse went about his business and no more was said that day. When George got home that evening, he explained to Hannah the conversation. Jesse's father had a lot of money, but Jesse was a good man. He knew he needed skilled men to work his mills. He was not concerned that they would become successful and challenge the lord of the manor.

Before anyone at the Manor House in the village of Saratoga knew anything about it, the little sixteen by twenty foot building was up. It took some time to get glass for the windows but everything else came from the hands of the fathers of the neighborhood children. As far as a teacher, Hannah said she would learn to teach herself if she had to. But it wasn't necessary. Eben found a young man named Steven Birch who was bright and anxious to become their teacher.[54]

That was how the little school near Toll's mill came into being. And that is why Tom Jewel at the age of six years, became one of the first Jewels to go to school on the property he eventually came to own.[55] It was the Jewel house and little school in the community we now call Grangerville. His brother and sister, James and Sissy, also got their first lessons at that little school. Hannah was happy that her children would be able to read, write and do their numbers. Now they would have a chance in the new United States of America . . .

Bobby joined States at the hotel and said eagerly, "I looked over those old papers that you had given me last night.

States paused for a moment, "Did you read them?"

"Most of it. It does sound like a wonderful way to live. Things must have been getting better for the nation then," Bobby commented, thinking of the tenements that he and his Irish friends in New York had lived in.

"Well, yes, until Napoleon messed things up in Europe," States started again.

"What do you mean? Messed things up in Europe?" Bobby asked. He knew that the French and English had a war many years ago but he didn't really put it into any context.

"Well, when Napoleon and England's war started in 1803,[56] we still did not have a real functioning national government. The Jeffersonian Democrats did not trust the Congress to establish an independent standing army. They fully believed it was just not necessary. However, our ships were being stopped at sea and sailors were being conscripted into service by the British

"Cargo was being impressed and any sailor that even looked British was snatched off the ships as a British deserter. Jefferson decided he must do something and so he requested Congress to pass the Embargo Act. You have heard of the Embargo Act haven't you?" States asked.

"Well no, not really. I know what embargo means, but I can't say I remember ever hearing about any act," Bobby answered.

"Well, did you go to school or did you just come over on a ship totally ignorant?" the old man snapped.

"I never was a real good student of history," Bobby admitted.

"Your editor really picked a fine young man for the job," States said a little sarcastically at first. Then in a softer tone . . . "well, it went like this. No one could legally ship anything anywhere in Europe or England. Of course, everyone ignored the act and became smugglers. They knew there was no army to enforce the new laws."

"This was where the trouble really started, when Jefferson needed to form a real army. None of the governors really cared about the new law. All they knew was that the embargo stopped trade and kept money out and smuggling brought it in.

"Officials did, however, try to accommodate the new law. A few army units were formed but the law finally was changed. The problems caused by the war, however, did not go away. Eventually something had to be done."

Chapter 9 - 1804 Burr and Hamilton

"On the morning of July 11, 1804, Alexander Hamilton and Aaron Burr raised their dueling pistols and took aim." Hamilton's shot was high but Burr's found its mark and struck Hamilton in the abdomen. Within 24 hours the former Secretary of the Treasury was dead. The State of New York and the State of New Jersey issued warrants for Mr. Burr's arrest. [57]

"Well, you do know Aaron Burr shot and killed Alexander Hamilton, don't you?" Old States growled.

"Yes, it was some kind of duel, I think," Bobby answered. "Hamilton had insulted Burr or something."

"It was a lot more than that," States went on. "Hamilton believed only the wealthy could rule the country. He often said as much. When it came to dispersing the native Indian lands, like the Mohawk lands here in Saratoga County, he said they should be sold in large parcels of five-thousand acres or more.[58] If smaller units were sold the common man, our old soldiers, might be able to buy them and then they wouldn't work on the large manors or in the factories. This was the view of many Federalists. Some of us even believed, that maybe they did want to bring back the king. We had won the war but the bigwigs said now we should get back behind the plow.

"Burr was different. He was a Jeffersonian democrat. He believed, like George and all the rest of us, that the common man should have the same rights as anyone else. George used to say, 'Old Cornel Burr did us all a favor that day when he shot and killed Hamilton.' He used to call Burr 'Colonel' even when he was the Vice President. He had known both Burr and

Hamilton from the time he rode with the Westchester County Militia. Colonel Burr was in charge of the line through White Plains in 1779. My uncle, John Jewel, was one of his dispatch riders that year. George was part of Lieutenant Baker's group when they built the Continental Bridge over the Croton River for Burr. After Hamilton came down on General Israel Putnam, 'Old Put,' you know. George never really liked Hamilton again.[59] Then that land stuff that really took Uncle George wrong . . . the soldiers all had been promised some land, but where was it? The war had been over for seven years, and still no land."

"What do you mean about that land stuff, States? I'll need more details on that," Bobby asked.

"Well, first it was the size of the lots for sale. Then it was the so-called "Incomplete Sale," but now I'm getting ahead of my story."

States started slowly. "I was about twenty-six years old when my mother had invited Hannah and her family over for a special Sunday dinner. We all enjoyed these events. It was a time when we could relax and hear about what everyone was involved in."

"The story, fresh on everyone's lips was about the duel. Those of us in the younger generation were much of one mind. Isaac was about twenty-four and he put it best . . ."

"I think the skimming little bastard got what he deserved," Isaac said.

"Hey, watch that language! There are young folks here," Hannah reprimanded.

"Well, he is," Isaac went on. "He was still angry about the Free Farm."

George spoke up. You are right to be angry, Isaac. The farms over on Livingstone Platt in Beecher's Hollow were anything but free. I know we only have three years left. Maybe when the final rental agreement is finished the timber rights and water rights will be withheld. If we can only use it to produce farm crops that will have to be okay, but it does have very good fields."

"From now on, we'll have to stay clear of Stephen Van Rensselaer and Alexander Hamilton's 'Incomplete Sale' offers. [60]

"Even though the New York Constitution forbids feudalistic policies, in New York the wealthy are still in charge of the sheriffs and courts. Fighting the system appeared to be futile."

Hannah said, "Isaac, you and your brothers were too young to remember what it was like during the war. And we knew both of those boys back then."

Susannah broke in, "We were all too young for what happened to us. You could say nothing bad about young Colonel Burr to my Isaac or your Uncle John during those times. We girls all thought it was terribly romantic when John told us Burr used to sneak over the river and go behind the lines to visit the woman he loved. Then he would be in command on the line the next day."

Susannah laughed when she thought about it. "We were all so young and naïve," she said.

Hannah spoke up, "Colonel Burr had made my brother, Abraham Buckhout, a captain in the Calvary.[61] George and Buck had a lot of good to say about the fighting skills of young Burr."

"That's what I mean," Isaac repeated. "When Colonel Burr put a bullet in that little bastard, he did us all a favor."

Hannah realized her sons had not lived long enough to understand how a person's experience colored what they thought and felt. "George, tell the boys why Hamilton and Burr were so different." She and her husband had discussed this many times as they had struggled to make the correct decisions for the family during those turbulent years.

George smiled and began to speak . . ." War changes men. We don't mean for it to happen, but when the fighting is over, every soldier is different. It is even a bigger change if the soldiers are basically children when it starts."

"Alexander Hamilton was only nineteen or twenty when the war started.[62] He knew his numbers so he became an officer of artillery. He was a courageous young man but a little arrogant. During the battle at New York City, one of his old cannons blew up and killed several men. That shook him a little.

"At the Battle of White Plains he was posted to the right of Colonel Graham and the Westchester County Militia on Chatterson's Hill. When the Hessians came across the Bronx River, he had to fall back like the rest of us, but the blame all went on Graham and our militia.

"George Washington took him on somewhat as a father. This didn't set too well with Old Put or his young assistant, Aaron Burr.

"When it looked like Old Put and his five-thousand man army were being abandoned in New York City, it was young nineteen year old Aaron Burr who led them north up the west side of the island in a running march to safety. Many of our friends were there. They all remembered the courage of Burr and Old Put in this action.

"A few days later, when George Washington left two-thousand and eight-hundred men trapped and taken prisoner at Fort Washington, neither Old Put nor young Burr thought he had done the right thing.

"In this way Hamilton learned from Washington, and Burr learned from Old Put. Two young men both experienced the war in a very different way."

It was Susannah who spoke next. "George is right. It was these associations that made these two men so different. However, I now realize it even was more. Neither of these young men had a normal loving father and mother like our Jewel boys. Will and Grandma Lizzy provided the stability we all needed."

"Isaac, I agree. Alexander was a bastard in the actual sense, but he succeeded because of his wits and intellectual knowledge. Aaron was an orphan who lost both his mother and father as a very young child. In a way they were quite alike. Both were scarred at a very early age. I think it was Aaron Burr's need for a mother's love that lead to his passionate love for his wife, ten years older than he."

"Enough of this talk," George said. "Isaac, you might be right. There is no doubt I would not like to return to Hamilton's lords and manors. I am through with life as a serf. If need be, we will sell our rights in the Free Farm and buy some warranty deeded land from our friends out in the military tracts. Now I want to take the young ones over to the pond and see if they can catch a few fish."

"With that short summary," States continued, "George had said what was necessary. It was a warm July Sunday afternoon. Alexander Hamilton was dead and Aaron Burr's political life was over. He would no longer waste his time thinking about them and that was that." Then he stopped talking.

"Well, that was what! What happened next? Who was right, Hamilton or Burr?" Bobby felt there must be more to the story.

States answered, "As George often said, 'It's not who was right, but what was right.' The War of 1812 proved to President Madison that the Federalist were right about needing a strong central government to protect the nation and a tax source to fund it. Jefferson was right. The common man needed to be protected by the Bill of Rights. Hamilton was wrong when he believed a preferential aristocracy was needed to govern a country and tried to keep the labor in the mill and the tenant farmer on the manor by not allowing the soldiers to buy land of their own.

"Burr was a good soldier. He was right when he demanded discipline. He was right when he opposed slavery. He was wrong when he couldn't forgive Hamilton.

"These men who are often called the fathers of our country were just men. They each had a few good ideas and a few bad ones. It was the men like George, and his boys, who fought against the bad ones and supported the good ones that built the country.

"Yes, of course, there was more to the story, but you and your readers have heard all that. Burr was crucified in the New York Press. He became the fall guy for all of those who hated Hamilton's view for the future of the USA, but Hamilton was dead. He could no longer use his intellect to tromp on the rights of the common man. The wealthy had lost their most capable orator," States continued.

"But what about George and Isaac's Free Farm?" Bobby asked.

"Well," States finished, "things had settled down after Hamilton's death. For about four years, life was good. Several of my children were born. George's youngest sons lived the idyllic life of rural boys who lived only a mile and a half from one of the prettiest mill ponds in New York State. George and the older boys at Jewel Bridge split their time between Toll's Mill, which is Grangerville and Jewel Corner. Harmon and Isaac managed the Free Farm on the Sacandaga."

Free Farm - Beecher's Hollow Map [63]

Chapter 10 - The Embargo, 1807

1807 – December 22, 1807 – "The Embargo," Thomas Jefferson, a Republican, Passed a Law making it illegal for American ships to sail into foreign ports, a sort of non-violent protest. [64]

The Embargo Act of 1807 . . . It forbade all international trade to and from American ports, and Jefferson hoped that Britain and France would be persuaded of the value and the rights of a neutral commerce. In Jan. 1808, the prohibition was extended to inland waters and land commerce to halt the skyrocketing trade with Canada. Merchants, sea captains, and sailors were naturally dismayed to find themselves without income and to see the ships rotting at the wharves. This caused the militia to be formed to stop the smuggling. [65]

States began, "The real problems didn't start until the war between Napoleon's France and England became heated and created real problems for American trade. Both France and England were impounding US ships, their cargo, and sometimes their sailors. Jefferson, with no good answers that worked, passed the Embargo Act."

"Did the Embargo work?" Bobby asked.

"No! It was a disaster for most people," States exclaimed.

"It stopped all trade. For George and Jesse Toll, the lumber market in New York dried up. This effectively shut down their mills. There was little left to do. Many people began smuggling potash to Canada for Great Britain's war with France. Potash, as you may know, is used to make gunpowder."

"As the New York farmers cleared their land, they burned the excess wood, then soaked the new hardwood ashes in water. Then, using the next fire to create ash, they boiled off the water and the brown cake that was left was potash. This product was sold to England through Canadian middlemen. The British used it to make gunpowder for the war with France. It brought a high price per ton, so it was an effective black market product."

"In fact, to stop this trade was partially why the New York Militia was called up in 1808. It was during the difficult times in 1808 that tragedy struck near the mill at Jewel Corner," States finished. [66]

George's son, Will, was running the small family mill at the time. He had gone into the woods alone that morning. It was a pleasant March morning when the sun came out and the crusted snow became difficult to walk in. The spring run-off would soon begin and there were still a few logs to skid to the sleigh road. All the easy timber along the creek had been cut several years ago. It was just the problem of cleaning up a few old trees with rotten tops. The trees that he planned to cut were not too big, so he would be able to use the one-man saw and his axe to do the work.

Will had been working for some time and the tree would soon be ready to come down. Will was a little worried because he had noticed some rot in the center of the cut. Just then a gust of the March winds moved his tree. It was just a little but he heard the distinctive crack as the tree broke too soon. The wind gently turned it around and it started to fall in the wrong direction. He abandoned the pinched saw and casually stepped behind the falling tree. It wasn't as if he had ever had the wind push a tree the wrong way before.

By then it was already too late. When he realized that the tree would strike a strong young oak sapling, he could not move fast enough in the slippery crusted snow to evade the dead branch. It was being flung in his direction by the supple young oak as if it had been shot from a cannon. When the branch struck Will, he only had time to utter a prayer. He fell unconscious and was fatally wounded to the ground.

When he did not come home for lunch, Sarah sent his younger brother, Tom, out to look for him. Tom had been getting the little mill on Snook Creek ready for the spring sawing. When he found his brother, it was clear that he was already dead. Tom ran back to Sarah and described the dreadful accident.

She told him to get Buddy, her brother-in-law, to help bring Will home.

States explained, "It was as if the whole world began to turn dark at Jewel Corner and Jewel Bridge.

"The markets had dried up with the boycott. Since Jesse Toll couldn't sell his lumber in New York, he shut down the sawmill on Fish Creek.

"With no money coming in, George moved the family up to Jewel Corner. He and the boys would farm the cut-over land. At least they would not starve. For the next several years the family struggled. The carpentry work in Saratoga Springs was the only bright spot for their little mill and their need for work."

Chapter 11 - The War of 1812

January 9, 1809 - "America passed the "Enforcement Act"; the shippers rebelled and broke the Embargo. [67]

March 1, 1809 - Jefferson signed a bill repealing the Embargo Act. Three days later his presidency was over and he left public life. He realized America would have to go to war or the Union would break. He gave up his last hope that the peaceful Embargo would stop England's abuses.

March 4, 1809, James Madison becomes the 4th President of the USA.

The Complete Non Intercourse Trade A with the belligerent nations was then tried. It didn't work either. Shipping just went through other ports as third parties. Trade boomed for a short while.

April 19, 1809 - An agreement was reached between Erskine, England and Smith, USA, to abandon the Orders of Council, so Madison canceled the Non Intercourse Act. Trade returned briefly in the fall of 1809 for four months. Then the agreement broke down again.

Winter of 1809/1810 - low prices for tobacco, cotton, and flour. The depression got worse as 1811 approached and Britain was blamed for it. People were starting to say that only war could make it possible to sell their products again. By July of 1811, people were saying that they would have to secure their trading rights by the use of the sword.

June 18, 1812 - War was declared and Published in New York, on June 20. The War of 1812 officially had started:

June 30, 1812, 10 days later; James George Jewel, enlisted - but he was discharged two weeks later, July 13, 1812. [68]

States continued speaking, "In 1812 war was declared but the only problem was that there was no national army, and the nation had made no preparations for war."

"What do you mean there was no national army?" Bobby spoke up. "How do you fight a war with no army?"

"Most of the armies all belonged to the states," States answered. "For example, ten days after war was declared George's son Jim joined the militia at Ballston."

Everyone was worried with all the talk of war. Early in 1812, George heard about the need for carpenters to build ships on Lake Ontario. By the time the summer work season was underway he had went north to build ships at Sackett's Harbor.

Hannah was especially concerned about her boys. They were all about the right age and ready to go. Even Harmon's little twelve-year old boy, Joe wanted to be a drummer boy or flute player like his older cousin had been in the Revolutionary War.

She did not know what Dan and Abe would do. They were working down by Yorktown, logging in the mountains somewhere. Will, of course, had already been killed in the tree accident, and Isaac was farming the Free Farm down on the

Sacandaga River with Harmon. Hannah was mostly worried about Jim, twenty-four, and Tom, twenty.

Hannah was grateful to Little Lizzy when she requested Tom to apprentice with her new husband as a blacksmith in Irvington. That job was badly needed and he would not be drafted into the militia. But there was no stopping her Jim because, within a few days, he had volunteered for the militia in Ballston.

Jim read the military order with excitement. It was what Betsey's brother Sam had said. He was sure they were all being called up. The War of 1812 had begun!

General Orders (GO):
Headquarters, Albany, 13th, August, 1812

In pursuance of a requisition by the authority, the President of the United States, the Fourth Brigade of detached militia of the State of New York, embracing that portion of the quota of the said State comprehended in the Counties of Albany, Saratoga, Greene, Delaware, Schoharie, and Montgomery . . . is hereby ordered into service to assemble and rendezvous respectively, on the 24th day of August, instant, by eleven o'clock, in the forenoon, in the manor and at the places following, vizt: that part of the said detached brigade comprehended in the County of Saratoga to rendezvous at the Inn of Zera Beach in the town of Ballston in said County . . . "

"Captain Waterman's Company of Artillery of Ballstown, in Saratoga County, will rendezvous with the Saratoga detachment, and will march from thence, under the command of Lieutenant Colonel Prior, and with his regiment. Brigadier General Dodge will cause the brigade to be mustered as soon as possible, and report the state thereof to Major General Dearborn at his headquarters, at Greenbush in Rensselaer County . . ."

"As the object of calling . . . to relieve a regiment of militia which has been in service at Sackett's Harbor and Ogdensburg . . . as to protect and defend our brethren on the northwestern frontier of this State. . . or cruel depredations of savages . . ." [69]

Jim thought he knew what the order meant. As part of the elite New York Fourth Division of Cavalry, they were being placed in the National Army as Volunteers. They would be subject to the Articles of War, as established by the laws of the United States. Major General Dearborn in Rensselaer County was in charge of the entire New York frontier.

It was already the sixteenth and that only left eight days before he would leave. He needed to find out what the local commander had planned. He might have even less time to prepare.

But no one he asked knew what was really going to happen. Everything was so disorganized. At first they held him only fourteen days and then sent him home. Now, would he be called up again for this order? But the call never came. When he went into town and asked, the officer told him the men had already been selected and he was not on the list.

The officer explained there just was not enough equipment, tents, cooking pots, muskets and ammunition to go around. So the men who had signed several years earlier and had more training were chosen to go.

One man, Lieutenant Kearney, was from the neighborhood. He had joined the regulars in the 13th Infantry Regiment that was formed up about the same time in Albany. Both Jim and his cousin, Buddy, had considered it but were too slow in going and the slots were full. The regulars also were not well-trained and lacked adequate equipment.

Jim was consigned to listen to the stories as they came back from the western front, at Niagara. Everyone was shocked when the militia refused to enter Canada at the Battle of Queenstown Heights, and a large number of American soldiers were forced to surrender. This fiasco was after they had succeeded in the attack and were in possession of the Heights over the town.

Lieutenant Steven Watts Kearney was taken prisoner with a young colonel, Winfield Scott.[70] The word was that Kearney would be recommended to receive a metal for bravery during the battle.

When Kearney came home to Gansevoort all the young men wanted to ask what it was like. Buddy, who knew him well, was especially taken and started talking about signing up with the regulars in 1813. Jim thought the Albany Volunteers were better equipped and better trained. So it was no surprise when they started to raise a new group of soldiers around February 15, 1813. Jim went with the Albany Volunteers and Buddy went with the 13th Infantry Regiment and Buddy had signed on with Captain Stephen Kearney.[71]

February 1813

Jim was excited as he loaded his equipment onto Star, a fine horse. States said if you chose to fight on a horse it must be a fighting horse. He often told how his father's horse, Shadow, had saved his life several times, and how his Uncle John's horse, Blackie, was almost a family legend. Jim was proud of Star, but he would not be fighting on horseback as he always had planned.

The horses would not be needed to garrison Fort Tompkins. In the winter they would actually be a liability. He would be considered as dismounted cavalry. So his friend, Jack O'Bryan, and he had agreed to be part of the Albany Volunteers. It was a well-trained and equipped group of two-hundred and fifty volunteers. The term, volunteers, did not mean they were not drafted. It meant they had volunteered to fight with the National US Army. They would receive no pay from the State of New York like the militia did. If they were to be paid it would have to come from the US Government.

Unlike the New York State Militia who could not be forced to fight outside of the USA, the Albany Volunteers had to agree in writing that they would fight wherever they were ordered to go. The lesson had been learned clearly at Niagara the year before. Militia could only be used to defend the new United States. They could not be used to invade Canada.

That's why Jim thought as a member of the Albany Volunteers he would be headed for battles in Canada. This was before he realized that now he would not go as cavalry. His mind went back to Star and that day last summer. . . .

69

Just then States had called him into the barn, and Jim could not imagine why . . .

There were several horses in the barn. Jim knew them well. He had trained and exercised them all. Star was the best and he expected States would get a real good price for him from some New York businessman.

States opened the conversation in his usual direct way. "Jim, you will need a new horse. It's time you give that little mare to Hannah and step up."

"There's nothing wrong with Jenny. She's sound and besides, I can't afford a new horse," Jim answered.

"No one said anything about you buying a new horse," States went on. "Remember how Uncle John always said you need the fastest horse. Well, that's what I'm talking about. Jenny is a fine little mare. She will be perfect for Hannah. But she is too small and too old for what you need. Your weight and your equipment demand a stronger horse, and I have just the one you need. Star here is three years old and noise trained, just perfect for the job."

"Sure he is. I noise trained him myself," Jim answered, "but he is your money horse this year. I heard you say so."

"Yes, you noise trained him," States went on, ignoring the bit about the money. "That's part of it. He trusts you. Remember when he was a colt? He was your favorite. You two have always bonded. A cavalry man's horse is his partner. My father would never forgive me . . . 'may his soul rest in peace . . .' if I sent you off to war without the best."

"It's your Pa who took care of us. It's because of him we live on this beautiful lake. Right now he is building ships up on the lake so the British will never get back to Saratoga where they stopped old Burgoyne. So it's not really your choice. It seems to be your destiny to get in the saddle and defend the country our fathers helped create."

With his little sermon over, States finished. He wanted Jim to understand when he went off to war, he didn't go alone but with the whole family behind him.

Jim stood silently in the entry of the horse barn, almost shocked at what States had said. Up to that point he had thought of the possibility of war as an adventure. Here was his older cousin whose had lost his father in the last war making it clear. The young soldier who just happened to be the right age did not go to war alone in some big adventure, but instead as the family's commitment to assure their fruitful future existence.

The lives of Jim's sister, Sissy, and his cousin, Maria, would in some way be guaranteed by what he and his partner, Star, would do during this war.

"Yes, I guess I know what you mean," Jim answered. He had nothing more to say. It would be years before he fully understood what his cousin was saying.

"Good. Now let's get a bridle on the big boy and see how you look on him, States said as he stepped into Star's stall."

"Feb. 4th, 1813"

"Johnathan Kellog of Saratoga County, Captain; Milton Bowers (Saratoga County) Lieutenant . . . another request for troops for Sackett's Harbor."

Feb.6th, 1813 Request from Major General Dearborn 3 or 4 companies of Volunteers into service of the U.S. at Sackett's Harbor. (Must sign a roll for at least sixty days). They will be allowed 2 days to go and 2 days to return."

"Rendezvous Monday, 22nd day of February." [72]

"Did you say your last name was O'Bryan, Bobby?" States asked.

"Yes, O'Bryan with an 'A.'" Bobby said.

"Well, you will like the next part of the story," States said as he went on.

"Jim and his friends, Jack and Sam O'Bryan, maybe family of yours, were sitting in the park adjacent to the Inn of Zera Beach in the town of Ballston. It was cold and windy but the sun was shining. Betsey O'Bryan, Jack's sister, had tears in her eyes and they were trying to tell her everything would be alright. Betsey was not only worried about her brothers but she was very fond of Jack's new friend, Jim Jewel."

Jim started to say, "It will just be a piece of cake," but he really knew better. "They say we will be taking Upper Canada this summer," he offered instead, sticking more to the facts.

Jack, still bothered by his sister's tears, put his arm around her and said, "Don't worry, I will look out for Jim and Sam."

"But who will look out for you?" Betsey blurted out through her tears. "Samuel is only sixteen. Why did he have to go?"

"I have to go because I am in the militia also," the boy answered indignantly.

"On Queenstown Heights the Indians killed and scalped boys who were just trying to surrender," [73] Betsey continued.

Trying to lift the mood, Jim interrupted, "Well, I guess we shouldn't plan to surrender then." All three young men laughed.

Jim could hear the Sergeant starting to call the men to order for the trip west. "We need to go now," he said as he picked up his gear and musket. Betsey put her arms around him and gave him a very warm kiss.

"Maybe we should reconsider this whole thing," he said as he came up for air. Betsey stepped back to be with her parents. And Jim turned to States and gave him a big hug and handshake.

"Be careful and look out for each other," States said as the young men walked away. He knew much better than they did as to what they were going into. This war was different. People said no one seemed to know why they were fighting. Maybe the New Englanders and the Canadians didn't know, but States was quite sure the Indians knew. The natives were what Hannah and his mother Susannah feared most. They remembered how the British had used the Indians to terrorize the small settlements on the Kayadrossera Patent. And how Johnson and his relative, Joseph Bryant, massacred women and children in parts of the

Mohawk River Valley during the Revolution. But nothing needed to be said about that now.

Jim had insisted that only States should go to Ballston to see him off and bring Star back home. His father was already up at Sackett's Harbor working on some new ships.

The cold February wind cut through the rendezvous area in front of the Inn at Zera Beach. The officers had assembled a string of big sleighs to haul the soldiers out as far as Little Falls where they would be assembled with other units. States, still holding Star's lead rope, turned and started back north to Saratoga Lake and a warm bed. As the road narrowed he was soon in the new little town of Saratoga Springs. There were already several hotels. He rode by Mr. Putnam's hotel and stopped by his friend, Mr. Holmes,' place for a warm lunch. He had worked on it as a carpenter only a few years earlier. Then he would go home to his farm and the evening chores.

Hannah was glad she had been able to say goodbye to Jim at home. The little ones could joke and hug him in the comfort of her warm home. She had always known that there would be no stopping Jim if war came. He always wanted to hear the stories of the Revolution, especially about his uncles, John and Isaac, and how they rode with Lieutenant Van Tassel and fought the Cowboys. He would swing his fake wooden saber and kill all the weeds along the roadside between the house and Jewel Bridge.

His Uncle John had told him, 'don't ever look forward to a war,' but he was too young to understand. Recently, they didn't see John and Elizabeth that much. Like all the young men of Saratoga County, Jim signed up for the militia when he was sixteen. He loved the camaraderie of the militia units, especially the cavalry.

But all Hannah could see when he came home with his new red uniform jacket a few months ago, was the five-year old little boy at the Bridge. He was very courageous. Dan had made a tricot hat and a wooden sword for him. He would step in front of the biggest team of horses and say, 'Stop! That will be two cents please,' holding up his sword. The teamsters had learned to expect it and would have the coins ready. 'Yes sir, Mr. Jewel!' They would shout and flip him the coins. As he grew older, and the younger ones took over the job even though he was still only about twelve, he would say, 'Stand up straight! Don't be afraid of the horses.' Both Tom and Sissy loved him.

His love of horses was nurtured by his cousin, States. In 1800[74] when States and his brothers moved down to Saratoga Lake and started raising horses in a serious way, Jim would walk down and ride the young colts to exercise them. He was twelve that year. Where had the time gone? Those years were Hannah's favorites.

Susannah was only three miles away with their farm right along the lake. Yes, 1800 to 1808 were her favorite years. How did Jim get from twelve to twenty-four so quickly? When the tree killed Will and Jesse Toll's Fish Creek Mill shut down because of the boycott, they had to move up on the farm. The Jewel Bridge tolls were nothing so they sold their house and interest in it before they moved north. Now George had to go north and work on the ships to fight the British. Finally this, her little boy in uniform was going, not riding off to war as he always had pictured himself, but instead, huddled under some straw in a large wooden sleigh just trying to keep warm. A bunch of young men, dressed in the green frocks of the Albany Volunteers, grasping their muskets and not sure what they were in for.

Hannah couldn't help it. The tears started to flow. She was glad her Sissy was outside splitting firewood and could not see her mother cry. She could not shut out the fear. The times she waited for George to come home flooded her mind. The worst was in 1777 when he had gone up to Saratoga. It was about three months and she heard nothing. All they knew was the British were coming down from Canada with a large army, like what may be happening now.

She knew that was why George had gone up to Sackett's Harbor to build ships. It wasn't just the need for money. He didn't want the British with their Indian friends murdering their way south again.

Hannah had told herself that she must be strong. Her family still needed her, at least a few more years. But today she wasn't sure. The orders were that Jim would muster up in Ballston and then go on to Little Falls. What then? The tears started again. But she took a deep breath. It was almost noon and her daughter would come in cold and hungry and full of life. She would be ready. She must be ready.

Bobby interrupted the story, "So you gave little Jim his horse . . . the one he went off to battle on?"

States answered, "Well, not quite. He wasn't little Jim anymore. He was Jim Jewel, a strong twenty-four year old man, and when the soldiers were called up that February of 1813, they didn't need the horses. They just needed men. In particular, they needed infantry and artillery men. Jim offered to give Star back when he found out he would not go as cavalry, but I declined. I told him, 'He's your horse and a man needs a good horse. He will be waiting for you here when you get home.'"

States continued, "Jim had the Jewel training in milling, woodworking and the forest, and if I can complement myself a little, he was also an excellent man with horses. Now can I get back to the story of the war?"

Bobby relaxed in his chair and said, "Yes, go on."

States started, "Well, the young men of Governor Tompkin's Army were quite a sight. They were called by some, 'The Albany Volunteers.' These units had been active since some time in about 1807. There was a reason for that. Regular militia usually signed up for about two weeks. The Albany Volunteers, when activated, were signed up for six months up to a year. They were fully trained and equipped. Some said, 'even better than James Madison's small Regular Army.' Unlike regular militia, the Albany Volunteers had to sign a paper that said they could be taken out of the country like the Regular US Army forces."

Bobby interrupted, "Is that what you meant when you said that there was no national army, just state armies?"

"Yes," States affirmed. "When they were called into national service they went without pay as volunteers."

"But they were real soldiers then?" Bobby asked.

"Well, they were all real soldiers, like regulars, militia and volunteers. But we all knew the Albany Volunteers were some of the best. Many of our local boys were involved."

"Lieutenant Ketchum, my stepfather's cousin, was in the artillery. He had a good education and was considered one of the best gunners in the state. They were soon all going to be tested."

Chapter 12 - Defense of Sackett's Harbor

"During May 1813 while most of our fleet was engaged in an attack on Toronto, Sackett's Harbor was poorly prepared for defense. Fort Tompkins was manned by about 200 dismounted dragoons under Colonel Backus, a detachment of artillery numbering 40 or 50 and 70 to 80 infantry invalids, recruits and parts of companies. A little east of the village was Fort Volunteer, a slight work erected by a company of exempts or Silver Greys" [75]

Jim and the O'Bryan boys were glad when they finally arrived at the military gathering area at Little Falls. They stayed there and trained more as they waited for the ice to clear out of Canada Creek and the Black River. Some of the men were dispatched to the headwaters of the Black River to build some bateaux, small boats, for the trip down river to Sackett's Harbor. Others built bateaux to move men on the Mohawk and some above the falls to send men up Canada Creek.

About the middle of April everything was ready. Young Sam returned with his militia unit to Albany. Jim Jewel and Jack O'Bryan went on to Sackett's Harbor with the two-hundred and fifty Albany Volunteers. General Brown's regiment of regular militia and about two-hundred dismounted cavalry men were already there.

It was near the end of April when they came floating past the small village of Watertown and around the corner into the lake at Sackett's Harbor.

"The first thing I am going to do after we land and unload, is look up Pa," Jim said to his friends, that is, if the Sergeant will let me.

"I'm sure he will let you," Jack volunteered, looking at the Sergeant close by in the front of the small boat.

"When everything is unloaded and we have completed the evening meal and, if you have not been selected to stand duty watch, maybe then," the Sergeant answered. "But you can't be hanging around talking to those shipbuilders. We need those ships as fast as they can build them. Does your Pa work on the ships or out at the sawmill?"

"I am not sure," Jim answered. "He is specialized in working with the mills and water power, but he also used to make special pieces for ships and boats in his shop."

"Find the foreman of the men working at the ship that you can see over there, and he may be able to tell you how to find your father," the Sergeant went on.

Jim was excited to find his Pa. It had been almost a year since he had left home. Since George could not read or write, it was only the occasional message the family got when they went over to Saratoga Village to pick up the family's share of his wages. The master shipbuilder, Henry Eckford, had made arrangements to pay the families locally through Mr. Schuyler. Otherwise, none of the men would go north and leave their families to starve.

Finally, everything was done, and Jim was released from duty about seven o'clock. It was a pretty evening but the breeze off the lake was very cool. The local men called it an offshore wind. The land would warm up during the day and air would rise, drawing the cold air off the water to flow ashore. Jim was interested in all the new things he was seeing these days.

"Your Pa is George Jewel, you say?" the foreman asked him.

"Yes, he is seventy-two years old. He builds and works sawmills," Jim answered in case the man didn't know him.

"Oh, I know George all right. Everyone around here knows him. He is one of the best men I have, but he doesn't look that old. I thought he might be in his late fifties," the foreman continued. "This time of the day you will find him in the Silver Grays' quarters. He likes to hang out with them. I guess if he is seventy-two he might have been in the big war with them."

"Yes, he was," Jim answered, thanking him for the information. He already knew where the Silver Grays were quartered. It wasn't too far from where General Brown had set up his Albany Volunteers.

Jim spotted his father sitting on a bunk at the far end of the long dark bunkhouse. He appeared to be deeply involved in a conversation with another shipbuilder. He slipped quietly up to within a few feet of his father who was facing in the opposite direction. "Pa," Jim spoke in his common everyday voice.

George Jewel's head jerked up and he looked at the young soldier standing before him. In disbelief he realized it was his son, Jim. "What are you doing here, son?" Of course, he knew what he was doing, but it still was quite a shock to see him.

"I'm checking on an old man who ran off to war, saying, 'I'm going up North to build a few ships. I will come home when I can.' That was almost a year ago," Jim teased.

"Has it been that long?" Pa stated in disbelief. "It only seems like a few months have passed."

By this time George was stood and hugged his son. Jim thought he could see tears well up in his father's eyes. Yet his hug was strong and rough.

"This fine looking young soldier is my son, Jim," he said to his friend. "So you joined the Albany Volunteers? I'm glad. When did you arrive?"

"Just today, a few hours ago," Jim answered. His father had recovered quickly from his little surprise.

"Let's go outside where the light is better so I can really take a good look at you," George suggested.

They talked about their families, the war and the "General Pike," the ship George was working on. It was a 28-gun heavy sloop of war. [76]

He told Jim how he had helped to build a local sawmill. His job was to keep the saws sawing and, when he had time, he would fashion special pieces for the ships or schooners. George had brought his own woodworking tools, but most of the men had not. They came up from New York City and expected the boss man to supply the tools.

Often some of the specialty parts were made in New York and sent north. When they arrived they were often the wrong size or just not the right part for a specific ship. Mr. Eckford soon heard that George could correct them or make a whole new item. With his fine tools he had made the wooden gearbox for the waterwheel. If someone could explain what was needed George Jewel could make it.

Jim was not surprised. He had seen his father lovingly make them a small fishing boat. It was not just an ordinary boat. It had ores but it also had a small sail. The little center board worked so smoothly, and as children, they just expected all boats should be as perfect. Now as an adult the crude boats that the army built had always left him dissatisfied with their function.

He also told his father that when he was leaving home around the middle of February, Buddy had signed up with Captain Kearney of the 13th Infantry Regiment of the US Regular Army. He should watch for him if the Thirteenth Regiment ever came to Sackett's Harbor.

They talked until the light began to fade. When Jim said goodbye, they promised to get together each week as long as Jim's regiment was in Sackett's Harbor.

In early May they heard the Americans had won at the Battle of York on April twenty-seventh. The word was that first they had occupied it and then they looted the town and withdrew to the mouth of the Niagara River. Here they began preparing to attack the British positions at Fort George.

At Sackett's Harbor the days passed quickly and soon it was near the end of May.

Bobby interrupted, "In May of 1813 the war had really erupted then."

"Yes," States answered, "although George and Jim didn't know it. On May twenty-seventh, Captain James Yeo, The British Fleet commander on Lake Ontario, was in a pitched battle with Captain Chauncey Squadron at Fort George. The British Governor General, Sir George Prevost, realized the US Admiral Chauncey's ships might be tied up there for several days. This might provide an excellent opportunity to take Sackett's Harbor and burn the 'General Pike' under construction there. This would shift the naval supremacy back to the British side on the lake.

"With most of the fleet engaged in an attack on the west end of the lake, this left Sackett's Harbor without ship cover. Fort Tompkins was manned by two-hundred of the 1st US dismounted dragoons, under Lieutenant Colonel Backus. And Lieutenant Thomas Ketchum's detachment of artillery, numbering forty or fifty, was manning the cannons." [77]

A little east of the village was Fort Volunteer with the Silver Grays. These men were over sixty and usually ex-

Revolutionary War soldiers. They built defenses and supported their sons in any way they could. The two-hundred and fifty Albany Volunteers at this time were camped on Horse Island.

The British set out on May twenty-seventh and arrived off Sackett's Harbor early the next morning.

With the first hints of light the alert was sounded. The watch at the Fort Tompkins had spotted the British sails. Everyone knew Admiral Chauncey's squadron was at the far end of the lake. If you were unsure you always assumed the sails were enemy ships.

Jim rolled off his pad with a start. "Jack, what was that?"

"The call to arms," his friend said. The men were piling out of their beds and pulling on their boots as fast as they could. In a few moments, what seemed like less than a minute or two, everyone was lined up in front of their tents.

Captain Herkimer talked to the Sergeant as the men lined up. "Attention!" the Sergeant shouted. "The Captain has something to say."

The Captain began, "The watch at the fort has spotted sails in the early morning light. They are coming this way. So we will be assigned here on Horse Island under Colonel Mills as we practiced last week. We will be backed up by General Brown's Militia and Colonel Backus' Dismounted Calvary."

Backus was the most senior Regular officer at the Harbor. This suited Captain Herkimer and his men very well because many of the Albany Volunteers were Calvary also, but they had been ordered out, equipped as infantry due to no need for horses.

Jim knew what this meant. They would be the first to face the British here on Horse Island. It was expected the British would land at Horse Island to avoid passing before Lieutenant Ketchum's guns in Fort Tompkins.

"If they had any sense they would not try that," Jim thought. "Ketchum's Artillery Unit was the best. They were formed in 1808 and had over four years' of experience."

When the British landed, the Albany Volunteers were to meet them and either drive them off or retreat back across the causeway and form up under Lieutenant Colonel Mills. Here Brown's Militia was stationed. They would hold there as long as they could, then fall back with the militia to the edge of the woods where Backus would be coming forward. Not counting the militia, with Backus' Regulars and their two-hundred and fifty Volunteers, their unit numbered close to four-hundred. Ketchum had about forty to fifty artillery men in the fort. There were also a few recovering wounded and invalids on the walls of the fort.

At first they could watch as the British landing party started for the island shore. Then the boats stopped.

One of the younger men said, "They are afraid. They are turning around already." The older men just laughed. They knew that wasn't true, but why had they stopped?

Soon, as they watched, the boats turned west towards Henderson Point. Jim heard the officers with telescopes say they could see a lot of Indians in these boats going west. It wasn't long before they could hear cannon fire from the British gun boats along with the flotilla.

"They must have found something to fire at," Jack realized. "Over there."[78]

"They were expecting some men from the 9th and 21st US Regular Infantry from Oswego. It must be them!" the Sergeant exclaimed.

Jim heard Captain Herkimer call to the Sergeant, "It will be dark soon. I don't think they will try to land this evening. Sergeant, send some men back to the cook tent and bring out equipment to prepare the evening meal. I think this evening we

84

will have a pleasant picnic in the woods along this beautiful lake."

The Sergeant laughed as he felt the relief. "Yes sir!" he answered.

When the evening meal had been prepared and consumed, Jim and his friends were told to improve their fighting position. They deepened their trenches along the island's shore and prepared a retreat path to fall back if they became outnumbered.

The Sergeant called the men together in the late evening light with his final instructions, "We will have no time to plan what to do tomorrow," he said. "As the British come ashore we will wait until we know our shots will all count. Than we will fire until we are forced back from the beach. Fall back with order but be fast. Crossing the causeway will be very dangerous. General Brown's Militia will be covering us at this time. We will form up there under Lieutenant Colonel Mills on the mainland."

"When we have to fall back again, get to the abatis and hold up. Find a good place to fire from. Just imagine a nice big buck is going to come walking down along that lake in a few minutes, picking his way through all those trees and sprouts cut down last fall. You don't want him to see you but you need to have a clear shot at him. Maybe a maple tree or a bunch of spruce branches will shade your position just enough to make it hard to see you," the Sergeant went on.

It seemed cold to Jim, planning how to ambush a man like a common deer. He had never killed a man before and said as much to Jack.

"You better get your head on straight and forget those ideas. It's him or you and I don't want to go home and tell my sister you were too dumb to defend yourself," Jack said harshly.

Jim was surprised by Jack's tone at first, and then he realized he was right. "I will," he replied. "I just hadn't thought of it that way."

"It's getting on towards evening and will soon be too dark to see," the Captain said.

"Pass the word. Remember your places! We'll be coming here early morning while it's still dark."

Then the Sergeant ordered, "Return to your tents and get whatever sleep you can. It's almost a certainty that the British fleet will be anchored right here off Horse Island in the morning."

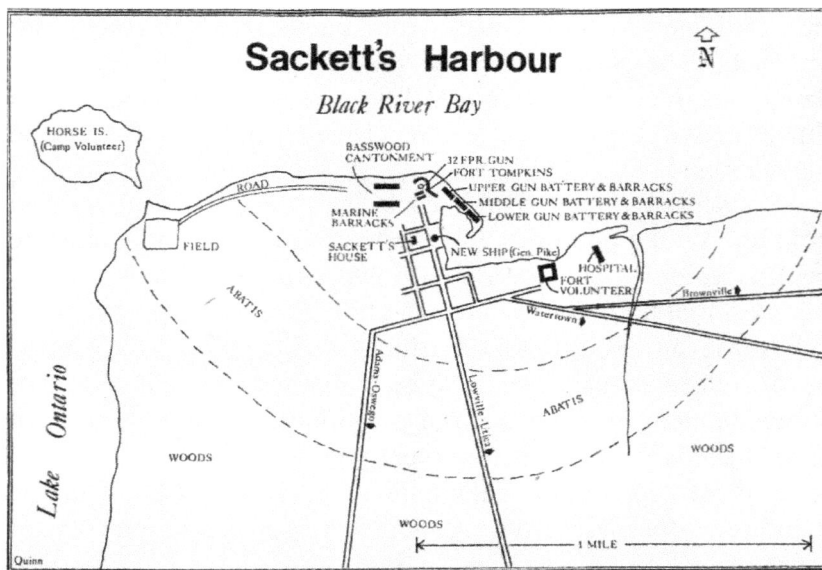

Battle Map of Sackett's Harbor [79]

As Jim lay in his tent, sleep was far from available to him. His mind ran over how the day had gone. Only seven boats out of the nineteen that had started from Oswego had made it to

Sackett's Harbor. The men in the rest of the boats were assumed scalped or prisoners. Their sacrifice had postponed the attack which will surely be expected tomorrow. Because of those who had died, Jim and many of his friends would live another day.

Jim thought of his father and knew where he would be. He would be with the Silver Grays polishing up the rifle he always took with him when he went into the wilderness. Jim heard that a few of the boat builders from New York City had walked the few miles east to the little village of Watertown on the Black River. They had said that their skill as boat builders was more important than dying as a soldier in a trench.

They may be right about this, but his father would stay there to support his son. The Silver Grays were a short distance east of the village at Fort Volunteer and that would be the location of his father.

Jim was right, of course. As George lay in his bunk, many of the old soldiers were talking. They had put pickets out in the woods to watch for Indians coming in from the south and east. These men were given tomahawks and pistols. There was no need for rifles in hand-to-hand fighting in the dark. There was no fear within this group. They all knew why they were there.

George thought of his son. He knew the Albany Volunteers were camped on Horse Island. It was expected that the British would come ashore there. The Volunteers would have to fall back across the causeway under intense fire. Their backup would be the militia on the mainland. But when the militia broke and retreated, as everyone knew they would, the Volunteers would need to move again. The militia with their hunting rifles would only be good for two or three shots when the British got close. The musket was much quicker to load. Equipped with the bayonet, it was deadly in close in fighting.

George knew Colonel Backus and his dismounted dragoons, probably about one-hundred and fifty regulars, were to march out and meet the British troops. The Albany Volunteers were to form up on their left and fall back with them to the Basswood Cantonment and trench works by the Marine Barracks.

The British field pieces would be firing at them from the front and Matthew's cannons would be firing over their heads from the Fort Tompkins wall behind them. It would take courage but he was confident that, of all his sons, Jim was probably the best for the job.

However, he had worked hard all day and nothing could keep his seventy- two year old body awake. Soon he was snoring gently.

The Captain's statements were accurate. As the first bits of light began to appear, the British gunboats were in their positions just off the shore. It was only a few minutes before the first shells began to explode. For Jim it was hard to hold fire until the signal was given. The first boats coming in from the west were within pistol shot before the order to fire came. Most of their shots found home. The British attackers seemed to shudder as the bullets found their marks. [80]

Brown's Militia were posted on the mainland where the causeway ended. They had two field guns raking the boats from the south. The British boats turned north to put the island between themselves and the militia field pieces. As they rounded the island, they came into view of Ketchum's big 32# gun on Fort Thompkins. Many of the attackers were coming ashore all along the north side of the island. When the number became excessive, Colonel Mills ordered the Volunteers off the island.

No one had to tell Jim or Jack to run when they left the Island. The three-hundred yard causeway was wide open and any British gunboat that could see it was firing at the fleeing men.

When Jim reached the small natural breastwork on the mainland beach, he looked around for Jack. "Are you alright, Jack?" he said.

"As far as I can tell," was the reply. Next to them were men firing one of the brass field cannons. They helped to reinforce the breastwork and dug in.

The Volunteers were located to the right of Brown's Militia right on the end of the causeway. [81]

The skilled British troops didn't stop on the island. As soon as they could form up, they began pouring fire on the militia both from their gunboats and muskets. They knew the regular militia units would only stand and fight where they had time to reload their rifles.

Brown's Militia, with their two field pieces and their hunting rifles, did significant damage in the first few minutes as the British troops came off the island. The fast charging attack soon broke the militia as they closed in on their lines.

Jim heard the sharp rifle crack . . . hundreds of them for maybe five or ten minutes at most, then only scattered firing. "The militia on our left have broken and retreated into the woods," he told Jack. "They won't face the bayonets."

"And well they shouldn't," Jack answered. Both men knew the limitations of hunting rifles in battle.

"They will be coming our way next. We need to get off this beach," Jim responded.

The British were within sixty paces when Mills ordered the Volunteers to fire. They got off three or four volleys before Mills ordered them to fall back. By this time the British were within fifty feet. When Colonel Mills stood up to give the order he was struck in the chest and died instantly. [82]

Although some of the native fighters followed the fleeing militia into the woods, the British Regulars seemed more inclined to pursue the retreating Albany Volunteers as they pulled back into the Abatis toward Colonel Backus' advancing troops.

When the British were coming into range, Colonel Backus was also standing and ordering his men forward. Almost instantly a bullet from some British musket cut the brave man down, badly wounding him.

But these men were not militia. They were US Army Regulars and Albany Volunteers. They fought on without their leaders. The four-hundred men were facing eight-hundred and fifty British soldiers.

> *It was later discovered that they were fighting Sir Prevost himself with the Grenadier Company of the 100th Regiment, two companies of the 8th Kings Regiment of Foot, four companies of the 104th Regiment, plus one company of the Glengarry Light Infantry, and two companies of the Canadian Voltigeurs and a detachment of Royal Artillery with two six-pound guns.*

Of course, Jim didn't know what he was up against. All he knew was there were about twice the number of British coming against them. When he mentioned this to Jack, he snapped back, "Just kill two of them."

He took this to heart and, instead of just firing into the crowd, he carefully picked out a man that appeared to be stuck in a tree branch. As his musket roared he saw the man flinch and go down. He stepped back behind his tree and carefully loaded his musket. This time he stuck his head out again and saw a man only about a hundred feet away. The man had not seen him until that instant. He quickly shot him right in the chest. The shock in the young soldier's eyes took Jim by surprise.

"Keep shooting!" Jim could hear Jack's voice over the din of battle. He must have stopped as he saw death in the young soldier's eyes. He quickly reloaded his musket as he remembered the Sergeant's words . . . 'just like you want to shoot a deer . . . ' Jim was about to search for another target when he heard the Sergeant's order. "Fall back! We need to give Ketchum more room to fire!"

Jim had noticed the American shells were exploding only a few yards in front of him. Jack was already starting to retreat when Jim caught up with him.

"Run for the earthworks near Fort Tompkins! I'm right behind you!" he shouted at Jack. The men ran as fast as they could as they crossed the open space in front of the trenches.

As they dropped into the trench they just looked at each other. "Did you get hit?" Jack asked.

"No! Did you?" Jim replied. Men were tumbling into the trench all around them.

"Load up and get ready!" the Sergeant shouted. "They will be here soon!"

But the British Infantry had taken a terrible toll by this time. Jack was right. In a way, if everyone could take two, the odds would soon be even. The fire was still coming from the infantry but the charge had stalled. Now from behind the revetment, volunteers and regulars were pouring heavy fire into the edge of the abatis where the advancing British had stopped.

All of a sudden Jim heard fire from the lake. A British ship had been pulled into range by some small boats, and it was pouring fire into Fort Tompkins. They had quieted Matthew's guns by driving him off the west wall, but they could not damage the Fort itself. Many of the shells were going over the Fort and falling on Navy Point, causing confusion. [83]

The attack had been stopped. General Brown could now be seen with the large number of militia that he had reorganized and were marching back into the battle. Provost decided the losses were already too heavy and signaled to retreat.

"They're leaving," Jim noticed. Soon it was evident and the entire group of surviving defenders began to cheer.

After a few minutes he sat down. He felt exhausted, as if he had run a hundred miles. The two young men just sat and looked at each other. They had survived their first battle. Not everyone did, however. Many of their friends were not in the trenches with them. When the firing had stopped completely they went looking for them. Some were wounded and some had already gone to meet their Maker. There were also wounded British soldiers. Now there were just boys or young men that needed help. How could that be? Only moments before they had been enemies. He had shot several of them—maybe killed some—maybe not. On the island he wasn't sure, but the last soldier still lay where he had dropped. Jim couldn't go near the body. Someone else would have to go and gather him up.

Bobby asked, "So Jim and his friend had been in a very dangerous battle. What happened to old George and the Silver Grays? Was their fort attacked?"

"No," States replied. "Before long, they were putting out the fires caused by the battle. Due to the confusion of the battle, some of the sailors had set the barracks and the 'Pike' on fire. However, in a few days things began to calm down again, and they all went back to work on the ships."

States went on as he often did when he was about to wrap a part of his story. "Jim told me later, at the second battle of Sackett's Harbor, Major Swan listed twenty-two killed, eighty-four wounded and twenty-six missing from the regulars and the Albany Volunteers, just about half of what the British lost. Their losses were later discovered to be forty-eight men killed, and one- hundred and ninety-five wounded and sixteen men are missing. Jack had been right. For every American killed, wounded or missing, two British were killed, wounded or missing."

"The British objective was not met. The ship, the General Pike, was partially burned, but since the wood was green the fire was easily put out. The ship was saved and quickly repaired. Later that year it had been used to defeat the "Wolf," another ship. And the Lake was ours for the rest of 1813."

"The British claimed victory but the Americans, for their part claimed that had Sir Prevost not retreated hastily when he did, he would never have returned to Kingston," States added. "Jim always said, 'in my first six months of the war, it was about one-hundred and seventy-nine days of boredom and one day of terror.' The real hero he insisted was his father, Old George, and the shipbuilders. Henry Eckfort and his crew built five ships, some in as little as twenty-one days, keel to launch. It was these ships that allowed control of Lake Ontario up until near the end of the war."

"Well, that is enough for today, Bobby. Fighting that battle again with Jim has made me tired," States finished.

Bobby knew he was being dismissed. "Again tomorrow at ten?" he asked.

"Sure," the old man answered as he started for the door with his white cane swinging.

Bobby looked over his notes. During the War of 1812 there was still only a small national army. President Madison had to beg the states for soldiers and they had to come as volunteers. "Who would go fight a war as a volunteer?" he wondered.

The real heroes were the old soldiers and shipbuilders who created a shipyard at Sackett's Harbor and built ships there. And also a few brave boys who were sent there to defend it.

Maybe tomorrow he could see what happened to Buddy who had gone off to war around the same time. "I wonder where he went . . . "

Chapter 13 - The 13th US Army in Canada

In the spring of 1813, "several detachments fought at the storming of Fort George, May 27, 1813, at which post it also served as a garrison unit . . . That fall the 13th Regiment ventured to Sackett's Harbor. . . It then sailed down the St. Lawrence River as part of General James Wilkinson's Montreal Expedition and fought at Crysler's Farm on November 11, 1813." [84]

"Good morning, States," Bobby called out as the old man shuffled onto the Hotel veranda. "How do you feel today?"

"Alright, once I'm able to stand up," States answered.

The young lady brought a sweet and some coffee over to the table. "Here is your coffee, Mr. Jewel," she said, as she slid the cup into his hand. The hotel manager had instructed his staff on how to treat this blind old man. Everyone liked him. She silently wished she could also sit down and hear the stories he was telling the young handsome New York reporter. Their meetings had become the talk of the hotel staff.

"I took the privilege of ordering us a little breakfast," Bobby went on.

"Thank you, Bobby, and thank you, miss," States replied as he gently touched the hand serving the coffee. After a few sips of the fresh coffee, States asked, "Well, where did we leave off yesterday?"

"You had just finished telling about George and his son, Jim, at Sackett's Harbor during the battle in 1813, I believe. I was wondering what had happened to old George's cousin, the one you call Buddy. You had said he enlisted in the 13th Infantry Regiment of the US Army," Bobby replied.

"Of course, now I remember," States began. "Well, during the summer of 1813, Captain Chauncey's fleet, with the General Pike, was the big man in the pond, as they say."

"Buddy's regiment was assigned under Colonel John Chrystie. At the same time Jim was defending Sackett's Harbor, Buddy was involved in the taking of Fort George at the other end of Lake Ontario."

Hannah checked often with Buddy's wife, Mary, and her young ones. With Buddy and so many of the men off to war, it was up to Mary and her to see to it that things ran rather smooth at Jewel Corner.

The mill was, of course, shut down. It was just as necessary to put in what crops they could and do the gardens. Her daughter, at twenty-two, could handle the chores for their two cows. It was also her responsibility to bring in the firewood. With her mare, Jenny, and all the slabs over at the mill, there was no shortage of dry wood. She just needed to find some overnight logs from the old oak tops along the creek.

Hannah was about her usual morning chores when she heard one of the neighbors shout something to her daughter who was working in the garden. It was mid-July and the weeds were growing faster than the vegetables.

"What did that man want?" she shouted out the door.

"He said there was a letter from Buddy at the post in Gansevoort," she answered. "Should I go and get it?"

"Well yes, of course. Bring it here and I will go with you to Mary's cabin and read it for her." Hannah knew Mary Jewel could not read. But Buddy had learned the basics of reading and writing from his father. His work for William at the mill had reinforced that somewhat.

It seemed like a long time before Sissy came riding back from the village. But when she did arrive she didn't come to the house. Instead, she pulled the saddle off Jenny and slipped the harness on. In a few moments she was in front of the house with the little one-horse cart.

Of course, the girl drove for her mother. It was about three fourths of a mile over to where Hannah's George had built the little cabin. It was originally built for their son, Daniel, before he moved back to Yorktown in 1798. Buddy and Mary came as newly-weds that same year. It was perfect for them.

When they pulled into the little farmyard, Mary's children were all lined up in front of the house. "Hello, Maria, Harmon, John, Betsey, Peggy, Benat and Herman," Sissy went on in her regular little ritual. The children loved it. The baby was just a year old. [85]

"How is it going, Harmon?" Sissy called to her cousin. They had grown up together. They often fished in Snook Kill sometimes played on the logs in the millpond when she was younger.

Harmon was thirteen years old. John was eleven. Betsey was nine. Peggy was five, Benat was three and the baby, one. "Quite a parcel of babies to leave with a young mother," Sissy thought. But Mary's husband thought they might get paid in land, and if not land, then the military pay was something.

"Mary, we have a letter for you. It looks like it might be from Buddy!" Hannah shouted to her young friend and relative. Everyone was so excited to see the letter. Hannah could see that someone must have helped Buddy to write the address.

> Mary Jewel
> Gansevoort PO
> New York

The Lieutenant had written the address for Buddy so that it would be very neat and legible for the postmaster. Of course, it needed to be, or it would not find its way into Mary's hand.

The young thirty-four year old woman took the letter in her hands and started to cry. She had only received one letter since that day on March first when her man had ridden off to war. And that one was very short and in someone else's hand.

"Why are you crying, Mama?" Little Peggy asked.

"I am happy your father is still alive." She knew Buddy's little Peggy would not understand but the older children would. She told Betsey to run into the house and bring out the butcher knife.

With the large sharp knife she carefully peeled back the lump of wax that sealed the folded paper. After she looked at the few words written in her husband's roughly formed writing, she handed the paper to Hannah.

"Please read it for me," she said.

By this time Hannah could feel the tears forming in her eyes also.

"My Dear Mary and Children," she started.

"We hope this finds you all well. It is the 4th of July and we all have the day off. My Lieutenant is helping me to write this because I was not sure how to do it. He said it was important for me to form my own words. I miss you all very much, especially having Peggy and Bernat giving me a hug before they go to bed. I am sure, Betsey, that you are helping your mother with the baby. She was so little, only a year old when I left. Harmon and John, it's up

to you to be the men around there. Be sure to shoot a deer once in a while and take good care of our cows.

And, of course, Mary, my loving wife, I miss you the most. Don't be afraid. I am taking care of myself. I wanted to let you know I did not even get a scratch at the storming of Fort George on May 27. We have been sitting around here most of the time since then. We did take a hike over to a place called Beaver Dam about a week ago, but for some reason we just turned around and hiked back. Well, the paper is full."

Love you, Your Papa and Husband

"PS, Canada is nice. I will have to take you up here sometime."

"Pa was there when they took Fort George," Harmon said. "That must have been something."

Sissy volunteered, "My brother, Jim, helped drive the British back when they tried to burn the ships that my Pa was making at Sackett's Harbor, about that same time". . .

Coming back to the present, States summed things up for Bobby, "These children were all proud of their fathers. To some the War of 1812 might have been a meaningless exercise. But to these two families, it was a life and death struggle."

"So, see if I have this right?" Bobby asked. "Buddy and the 13th Regiment of the US Infantry were in Canada taking

Fort George, just north of Niagara Falls at the exact same time that Jim was defending Sackett's Harbor. That's why they didn't have ship cover from the lake side."

"That's right," States affirmed. "You seem to be learning," as he gave a little chuckle.

"What happened next with Jim at Sackett's Harbor?" Bobby asked.

"Well, I was just going to get to that," States continued. "Jim and his friend finished out their six-month enlistment about the middle of August with no further action. They were released and marched home. Jim used to say it was just a pleasant summer hike in the woods."

"In fact, the overall experience was so pleasant, that a bunch of the young men decided to re-enlist for three more months. They were told to keep their equipment and then given a few days with their families. They were fully equipped even with their Red Jackets of the New York State Cavalry. This time they would actually go as cavalry. They would be attached to the 5th New York Volunteer Cavalry under Captain Wilcox. [86] Most of these men were from Columbia County. There were only about forty troops from Albany and Saratoga under their special three- month enlistment. As Cavalry they could be moved quickly to the Niagara Frontier."

Chapter 14 - Escape at Fort Niagara

"In late 1813, Major General Francis de Rottenburg, the British Lieutenant Governor of Upper Canada, had been alarmed by defeats in the west (the Battle of Lake Erie and the Battle of the Thames) and American concentrations to the east, and on 9 October he ordered the troops on the Niagara Peninsula to retreat hastily to Burlington Heights at the western end of Lake Ontario. He intended to abandon even this position and concentrate his forces at Kingston but during the first week in December, de Rottenburg was replaced by the more forceful Lieutenant General Gordon Drummond who was aware that the American attack on Montreal had been defeated, leaving the American Army stranded in poorly-supplied winter quarters in Upper New York State. Drummond immediately cancelled de Rottenburg's plans for further retreat, and ordered the units at Burlington Heights to advance instead." [87]

Jim and Betsey were sitting in the pretty little fishing boat that the Jewel family owned. They kept it tied up by Saratoga Lake these days. States' boat, and several others, were all kept in the same place. It was on the north side of the lake, opposite Moon's Landing.

"Do you really have to go back? "Betsey asked. "Wish you had considered how I would feel having you stop by for a short visit and then off again to war."

"It will only be for three months and our ships control Lake Ontario," Jim answered. He was quite confident that all of Upper Canada would soon be in American hands. "They needed a few men that could move fast to garrison the forts near Buffalo. There must be something big afloat," he explained.

He couldn't really make his feelings clear, but it was as his father had said, 'When you go to war, somehow you become part of it, instead of the other way around.'

"You wouldn't want me to stay home while your brothers go off and fight to keep us safe," Jim answered. Jack had warned him earlier that she might want him around more, when he said, 'You'd better be careful or soon we will be related.'

Jim looked at the beautiful girl in the boat with him. The sun glistened on her pretty red hair. Her blue eyes sparkled like diamonds. Well if he was to be captured and end up married, he couldn't think of anyone better than Betsey O'Bryan to do it.

"You are very quiet," she said. "What's on your mind?"

"I was just thinking how beautiful you are." His declaration caught her off guard and she blushed. "See," he said, "you don't even know it."

She leaned forward and gave him a kiss. "I'm a sucker for a soldier in uniform," she giggled.

"Yes, I know. That's why I'm wearing it." They both laughed. "I better get you home before I completely have you in my grasp," Jim said as he picked up the oars. Neither of them wanted the day to end, because it would be their last private time together for three months.

In the morning Jim would be forming up with Captain Wilcox and heading out. Some said they may be going to relieve the men in Fort George. It was on the Canadian side, just north of Niagara. This was a job for the Albany Volunteer Cavalry, Red Jackets and all.

There was a small crowd in Ballston to see them off. The officers had set the departure time for 10:00 in the morning so all the families could be in attendance.

This time Hannah had Jim drive the whole family down in the large mill carriage. Star was tied and walked slowly behind. There were a lot of tears. Harmon and his brothers and sisters were very excited to see all the soldiers. Even Little Peggy said goodbye to her Uncle Jim. Then she enthusiastically waved her little hands as he climbed on Star and prepared to line up with Jack and the others.

It was all over too quickly for Hannah. She knew the count of soldiers lost at Sackett's Harbor. One out of five of the Albany Volunteers came home wounded or didn't come home at all. Hannah didn't try to stop the tears, but Susannah noticed and put her arm around her. "It will be alright," she said. "It is only three months." But neither was sure. They would be right near where so many of their first group of boys suffered such high casualties at the Battle of Queenstown Heights.

"Let's not dawdle here," Hannah said. "Let's get back to your place and have some dinner." Both women smiled wearily.

"Marie, gather up the little ones," Mary said.

"Sissy, hook the team back up to the carriage so we can get started," Hannah ordered. For her it was important to keep focused on her little clan. Susannah, Mary and her seven made eight, plus Sissy and Hannah made a total of eleven.

Hannah pulled the carriage in line behind Susannah's family wagon and they all started north. There were a number of other families going in the same direction. "It looks like a caravan from the Bible," little Peggy said.

"Yes, with God watching over us," Hannah agreed. It made her feel better to remember God could watch over Jim and Jack as well. She shut her eyes and asked for their protection. The carriage slowly bumped along the road to Saratoga Springs and to Susannah and her son's farm.

103

Jim and Jack sat leaning against the wall of Fort George eating their evening meal. It was mid-October and they had only been here about a week. The American regular and militia troops, under General James Wilkinson, had been ordered by Secretary of War, John Armstrong, to march to Sackett's Harbor and prepare for an anticipated attack on Montreal.

The big lake kept the air mild and the soldiers' duty was very pleasant so far. Their only worries were that the British army was not far away and there were numerous Canadians Renegades who apparently had chosen to fight on the American side in camp. There were also a number of people who identified themselves as militia, but Jim thought many of them were just scoundrels because they were undisciplined and seemed to wonder around at will.

For these reasons the horses were kept near their tents and always under guard. Many of the buildings were gone, burned with hot shot when the fort was taken a few months earlier. Some of the buildings had been repaired but the small Albany Volunteer Cavalry unit preferred to stay close to their equipment and mounts.

"It's strange," Jim said, "that Buddy and the 13th US were living right here in this very same area. I was talking to a local man who delivers vegetables. He said he didn't remember any Buddy Jewel but he only got to know a few of the men."

"I heard some of the men have been catching nice pike and bass off the dock where they bring the supplies in," Jack said, changing the subject. "Maybe we could get an evening off and give it a try. I always keep a little fishing equipment in my pack for emergency."

"The Irish must be similar to the Dutch then," Jim replied. "I always have a few special items for emergency in my pack also. A good sharp knife about a foot long, a flint and steel for fire, and some line and fishing hooks. Pa says, 'if you starve in the woods of New York it's just because you are too dumb or too lazy.'"

"I didn't know you were Dutch. I always thought Jewel was an English name," Jack replied.

"It may well be. But our family lived in the Dutch part of Westchester County, just north of the city. We've married into the Dutch families for so many years so we are now basically Dutch. In the Dutch language, Jewel is spelled J-u-e-l," Jim explained. Jack was easy to talk to and he would make a good brother-in-law if Betsey would decide to marry him.

"I wonder what this General McClure will be like. I see he is one of our state officers but I haven't heard much about him," Jim went on.

"He sure doesn't ask for much discipline," Jack replied. "I think we are an accident just waiting to happen."

"The Sergeant said that very same thing this morning," Jim offered. "That's why he set up the continual watch on the equipment and horses."

Jack agreed, "That Captain Leonard seems worse than the General. Last night I noticed he left the post and didn't come in until this morning."

Later in the first week of November, Jack was fishing as he often did. There was activity on the American side of the river. He soon realized what was causing the commotion. It was the arrival of General Harrison and his so-called reinforcements from the Detroit frontier. Soon a crowd had gathered at the dock to check out the new arrivals. It was nearly dark as the final men came ashore. Now the expected adventure to the west could be undertaken.

By the fourteenth of November, Harrison's Regulars and the militia units had nearly completed preparations for the attack on Burlington Heights. But on November 15, the very next day, Commodore Chauncey arrived with ten ships, and

Harrison and his troops just loaded up and left for Sackett's Harbor.

McClure called an emergency Council-of-War of his staff and regimental commanders. Their decision was to march out with all the men he could spare to attack the British troops just a little to their west.

A few days later, on the evening of November 25, a bitter cold set in and froze the ground. Colonel Wilcox called the men together for an inspection of the horses and equipment. "Tomorrow we will ride against the British on Burlington Heights," he said. "Our unit will scout their forces and report back to the General. We will not engage. We will, in all probability, be seen but we do not expect that they will have cavalry to pursue us. If they do we will retreat. Any questions?" he asked. [88]

"What time will we leave?" the Sergeant asked.

"Have the troops ready to ride at dawn. Anything else?" he answered. "Okay then, get some sleep and good night."

"I should have asked, 'Why did we have to wait until it got so darn cold?" Jim ventured.

"Yes," Jack answered, "and he would have said, 'Sergeant, get that man's name. My horse needs to be curried tonight before he goes into battle.'"

"It will feel good to be riding again anyway. I sure am tired of sitting in this burned out old fort and doing nothing but chores," Jim replied.

"Tell me that tomorrow night," Jack went on. "Maybe by then, doing chores will look really good."

"How did the battle go, States?" Bobby asked. "Well it didn't," States answered. "The following morning, Colonel

106

Wilcox with his two-hundred mounted troops, including Jim and Jack, had pushed on ahead to scout the enemy's main line positions. They were looking for weak points that could be exploited the next day.

"By evening, Colonel Wilcox's detachment returned with the following information. It was apparent that the British had decided not to wait for McClure's assault. They were moving east with a force of between two and three-thousand men to meet his forces head on.

"The officers called a quick council and decided to wait until morning to determine if they should make a stand or return to the fort. By morning the desertion of nearly half the force, between six and seven-hundred men, made the point mute. Empty tents, abandoned rifles, and missing horses made it very apparent that the militia did not think to stand and fight was a reasonable option.

"With less than a thousand men, McClure hastily retreated to Fort George where he went through the motions of preparing for the expected attack by the advancing British force. But his heart was not in it.

"Militia men, who well remembered those trapped up against the river on the Queenstown Heights, demanded their discharge. Their term of service having expired, it seemed a very good time to go home.

Jim used to say, 'It seemed cowardly but their analysis was correct. They would not be able to stand, out-numbered three to one, and the British with muskets and bayonets up against their hunting rifles.' Some of the older men remembered just how ineffective these tactics were during the Revolution."

States summarized the situation for Bobby. "Neither of the young men knew what else was going on around that same time on the other end of the lake."

"During September and October, General James Wilkinson had been pulling men together at Sackett's Harbor for an expedition into Canada against Montreal. The 13th Regiment of US Infantry was with him."

"You mean Jim and Buddy had actually switched places from where they had been in May?" Bobby interrupted.

"Yes," States went on. "It was strange but that was exactly what had happened. On November 11, in 1813, Wilkinson's Expedition against Montreal stalled and then was defeated in the Battle of Crysler's Farm.

"About that time, a new and more aggressive commander took over in that part of Canada. He knew Wilkinson had gone into winter quarters in a poor location in upstate New York. He changed the earlier plans to vacate Niagara, and instead of withdrawing from the Niagara area, he ordered an advance.

"General George McClure, at Fort George, heard of the Canadian's revised plans and realized it would be impossible to hold Fort George on the Canadian side of the river. He only had a few men left to him, sixty regulars, forty of Jim's Albany Volunteer Cavalry and around one-hundred renegade Canadian Volunteers who had chosen to fight for the United States. This was not enough to hold Fort George and McClure knew it. [89]

"The majority of Colonel Wilcox's Cavalry, the one-hundred and sixty men from Columbia County were part of those whose enlistments were up. Wilcox left a lieutenant in charge and took the main unit home. It was apparent to him that there was little that could be done to keep that many horses alive with no provisions now that the snow had started.

"Jim and the forty troopers, who had joined with him at Saratoga, were instructed to return home when their enlistments were up in about a month. Colonel Wilcox was adamant and cautioned them. 'Don't try to stay! You will starve your horses and be of no use to anyone!'"

What happened next would haunt Jim for the rest of his life. He used to say that he often 'saw the burning homes and little children in his dreams.'

The Secretary of War, Armstrong, had given tentative orders, that if Fort George had to be abandoned, it and the surrounding supporting village should be destroyed, thereby making it uninhabitable for a British garrison.

On December 10, 1813, in a somewhat panic situation, General McClure realized he would have to abandon Fort George. He gave the order to set fire to the fort and the surrounding community of Newark. He thought it was quite clear that women and children should be given time to care for their needs.

The problem arose when the Canadian Renegades and some of the most destitute and lawless militia were given the job. The situation soon became a disaster for the local Canadian village residences.

"Help me pull this cart to the dock," Jack asked as he hooked his horse up with a makeshift harness.

Jim brought Star over to help. The horse was skittish in his rope harness but he trusted Jim and didn't buck. As they arrived at the dock where some other men were loading the supplies in small boats, Jim looked up. "What are those fires?" he yelled.

"Some of the men were instructed to burn the town," a man at the dock answered.

"Burn the town!" he repeated as if he couldn't believe his ears. "Who would order such a thing as that?"

"The General," the man replied.

"Maybe they are only burning public buildings," Jack answered.

"I don't think so," Jim went on. That section over there is just private homes. I met a nice family over there on our patrols. I'm sure that is his house in flames. He has several children."

Jim sat down in disbelief. The bitter wind whipped around his face. "How could this be done?" He thought. "Are we animals now, with no feeling?"

By morning, as the last of the supplies were being taken over to Fort Niagara, he could see the pitiful site clearly in the morning light. Small groups of women and children were huddled around the burning remains of their homes, trying to stay warm.

"We will pay for this," he told Jack. "We will pay dearly for this. God will see to it, and if not God, those children's fathers will."

"I think you are right," Jack sadly replied. "I am not a religious man, but I don't think you can treat God's children that way and escape untouched."

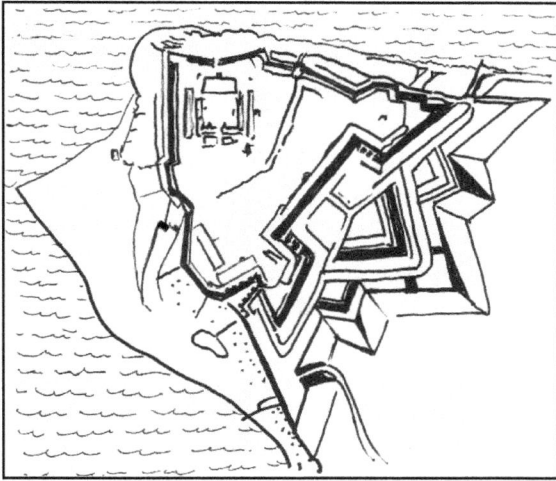

Plan of Fort Niagara

God's retribution didn't wait long, as Jim had suggested, it came from the hands of the children's fathers and a man named Colonel John Murry.

Fort Niagara, on the American side of the river, was a big place. It was quite old and had been built for just under a thousand men. On the night of December the eighteenth, there were approximately four-hundred men in Fort Niagara's garrison. Some were in the hospital. Most were asleep except for a few sentinels left to guard the fort. Captain Leonard was home, and miles away from his post.

Jim's lieutenant had selected a location for their camp in the northeast corner of the fort. It was about as far from the gate as he could get.

Since they would be leaving within the month, they slept in what was left of one of the old wooden buildings. The horses were picketed right behind it. Everyone was told to keep the horses out of site as much as possible. The quality of the men in the garrison had not improved and extra security was necessary. There was a watch posted with the mounts that changed every two hours because of the cold weather.

There were only about sixty regulars and the forty Albany Volunteer Cavalry who could be trusted. The one-hundred Canadian Renegades were a despicable lot. Jim found out they had been responsible for the looting and the rough treatment of the Canadian civilians. There were perhaps two-hundred of the local militia who were rough frontier folks with very little discipline. They seemed to come and go at will and many were heavy drinkers. [90]

Jim had just finished the 12-2 watch and was huddled by the stove trying to warm up. He was about to take off his coat and crawl under his blanket when the man who had just replaced him burst through the door.

"We are under attack, I think! I heard several terrible screams and then, quiet!" the guard frantically told the Sergeant.

"Up, men!" the Sergeant shouted. "Only pistols, sabers and daypacks! Get to the horses!"

Jim shook Jack awake, who was too groggy to comprehend the order. "Wake up! The British are here for their revenge! Hurry! I'll saddle our horses!" he shouted, as he grabbed only what the Sergeant had suggested. They had all expected an attack after the disgraceful burning of Newport, and here it was.

Jim and the other posted guard were the first to the horses. He could hear the carnage going on at the main barracks. The gate was obviously open. As he suspected, he could see Indians running for the horses in the moonlight. He threw his saddle on Star and was just finishing Jack's mount when the first natives were upon them. The pistol was useless so he stuck it in his belt and used his saber to deflect the first stroke of a war club.

He swung onto Star in one motion. Fighting on horseback gave him a height advantage from war clubs and tomahawks. The two mounted men silenced the two Indians who had focused on killing them. Instead, some were trying to get horses loose on the other end of the picket line. Men were pouring out of the old wooden bunkhouse. They had not yet been discovered by the attacking British soldiers.

"Here, Jack!" Jim shouted. He had kept Jack's mount with him so some other soldier didn't grab him.

"Thanks!" Jack said as he swung into the saddle. All he had on was his boots, pants, coat and saber.

The few Indians who were after their horses were quickly driven away by those already on horseback. The natives who had hastily secured a prize quickly melted into the darkness.

"Sergeant, get these men out the gate! If you break free, ride with great haste to the headquarters at Camp Buffalo and tell them the fort has been lost!" the Lieutenant ordered. [91]

There were perhaps half of the troopers on their horses, most without saddles, some even without bridles. But every man had his saber in his right hand.

"Ride, men!" The Sergeant shouted.

In the moonlit night, the horses galloped across the snow-covered parade ground of Fort Niagara at a fierce gallop. The herd instinct of their mounts was in charge. Jim, Jack and the other men who had succeeded on getting their mounts saddled, were in the front to guide them. The rest just followed.

Most of the attacking forces were already through the gate when the charging herd of horses burst through. Any one close enough to challenge them was met with a saber blow. The British instructions not to fire actually assisted them in their escape.

As they rushed out onto the road, musket shots began to follow them. The Sergeant didn't rein the troop in until they were well out of range. They waited a few minutes for the Lieutenant and the rest of the men, but it was soon evident they would never come.

"The Fort has fallen!" the Sergeant exclaimed. "Our orders are to ride to the headquarters at Camp Buffalo to raise the alarm! Share your weapons and clothes if you can spare any."

They carefully evaded the British troops in the small village of Youngstown, and then rode at a swift gate to Buffalo. By late afternoon on December 19, 1813, the small contingent of Cavalry rode into Camp Buffalo with the news. Fort Niagara had fallen and an attack on Buffalo was anticipated soon.

Later, it was learned that the attacking force numbered five-hundred and sixty-two and was under the command of Colonel John Murray. They also burned Lewiston that next day and a number of farms in the vicinity.

The Sergeant, along with Jim and Jack, were made part of a mounted patrol under command of Lieutenant Broughton. For the next few days, they watched and patrolled the shoreline between Black Rock and Buffalo. On December 29, 1813, the expected attack came.

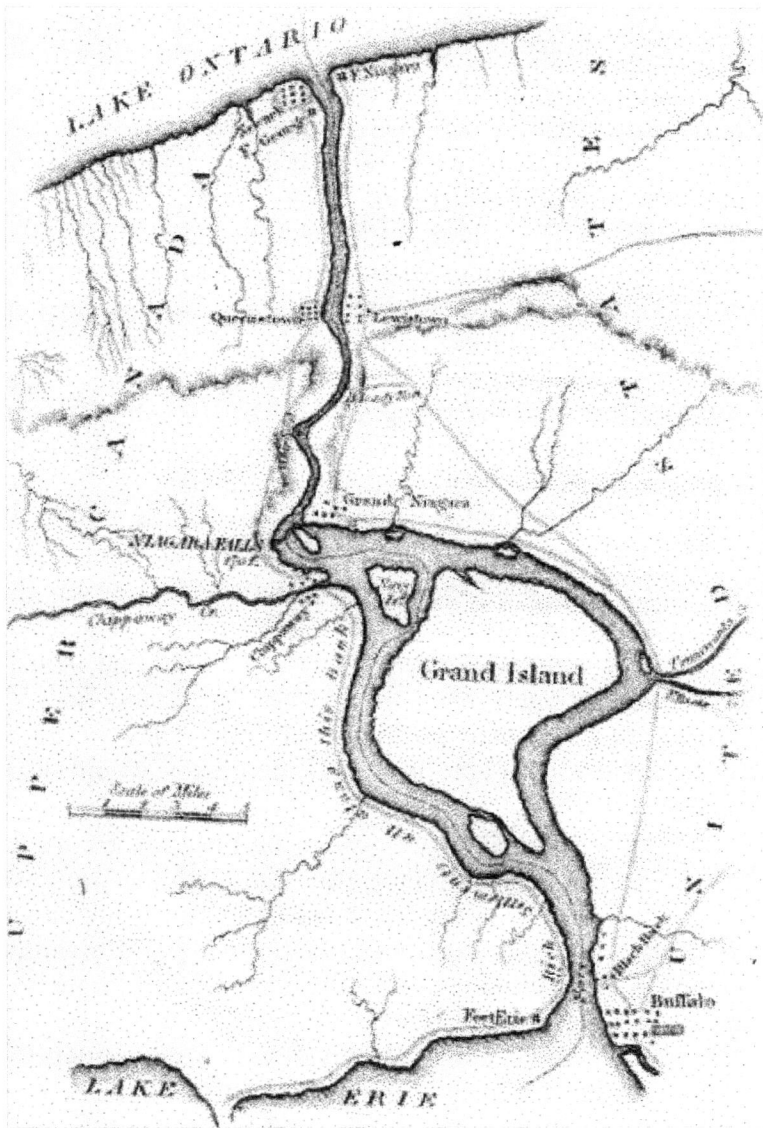

Map of Buffalo and Back Rock[92]

Just after midnight, on December 29, Jim and Jack were riding north when they heard the shots. "That sounded like rifle fire over near the lower battery by the creek!" Jack exclaimed. The small patrol of five men rode north to investigate.

Jim was the first to see the size of the invading force. "It's quite a large force," he whispered.

Lieutenant Broughton, attracted by the firing, soon arrived with the remainder of the patrol. He advanced to the position by the creek where Jim and Jack had stopped and observed the enemy action.

"A significant number of men, perhaps thirty, surprised our battery. That was the firing we heard. But I think the few men there have surrendered. The main attacking force is still north of the creek," Jim explained to the lieutenant.

"Thanks," the lieutenant quickly responded. "Sergeant, send two men back to headquarters and tell General Hall at Buffalo the attack has begun. We will try to slow up their progress a little here." [93]

The little company of cavalry bravely fired and then fell back, only to fire again from what cover they could find. The rifle flashes revealed their position each time. They would fire where the last flashes came from and the enemy would do the same.

Each time Jim selected a new firing position. He tried to position Star in a protected place also. Although the fire power was small, it had the desired effect that a skirmish line always has. It made the advancing troops slow down and use caution. The enemy was never quite sure in the dark where a larger army might be hidden.

By dawn General Hall had arrived with his men. Artillery shells were coming from across the river. The Regulars Army and Albany Volunteers units fought well but the militia broke, having no fortifications from which to fight.

General Hall later said in a letter to Governor Tompkins:

> *"The whole force now opposed to the enemy was, at most, not over six hundred men, the remainder having fled in spite of the exertions of their officers. These few but brave men disputed every inch of ground with the steady coolness of veterans, at the expense of many valuable lives.*

> *"Deserted by my principal force, I fell back that night to Eleven Mile Creek, and was forced to leave the flourishing villages of Black Rock and Buffalo a prey to the enemy, which they have pillaged and laid in ashes."* [94]

Jim knew this battle was not going to end well when he realized there were so few of the militia infantry men with the General.

"Where are all the men from Camp Buffalo?" he asked Jack.

"I don't know. There were two-thousand men there only a few days ago," Jack replied.

"It's just as the old regulars have always said, 'Without fortifications and a reasonable chance of success, many will not stand and fight,'" Jim explained.

"Do you blame them?" Jack answered. "Their wives and children are alone on some little farm in the woods waiting to be scalped by some of these Canadian Indians. They are not cowards. They have just made another choice. It makes more sense to leave before the battle, than during it, with a wild Indian chasing you waving his tomahawk."

Jim liked how the 'Irish' in Jack could see the poor man's position so clearly. It probably came from all the evils his people had always suffered from the British in his homeland. "Ideas like that stay in a family for a long time," Jim thought.

"When we fall back, as we will be doing in a few minutes, we, at least, have our horses to make an escape. How brave would you be without Star here today?" Jack had barely gotten the words out of his mouth when the order came to fall back. The Cavalry would again be used in the rearguard. Their mobility made it the most reasonable group to use.

As evening was coming on Lieutenant Broughton's little company of Cavalry rode silently into the evening camp at Eleven mile Creek. It was over four hours since the last pursuing natives had given up the chase. Jim was dead tired. He had been in the saddle since midnight. Star was also very tired and in need of rest and some food. With no ceremony the men quickly fed their animals and hit the blankets.

With only one day of rest Jim woke up on New Year's Day, January first of 1814. He half expected to be ordered back west to Black Rock to try to force the British back across the river. So he was quite surprised when Jack came running up all excited.

"What has you running so fast this morning, Jack?" Jim asked.

"I have just finished talking to the Sergeant. Remember how our enlistments expired last night? Well, the Sergeant talked to the lieutenant and the colonel. He told them what Colonel Wilcox had said about not starving our horses by keeping them on some under-supplied wilderness front over winter. Well, the officers all agreed by saying that, what is left of our Ballston Saratoga Cavalry unit should go home and recuperate. Word came in that the British were afraid to stay at Black Rock and had gone back to Canada. Some of the Indians had continued burning the abandon homes but that was not a task for cavalry. So! We are going home!" Jack shouted in excitement.

At over forty miles a day they were in Ballston by January 5, 1814. Now they were civilians again. This was the same day that General Hall was put on trial.[95]

Jim replied, "Tell Betsey I will be over to see her the day after tomorrow. I need to let my mother and family know I'm home safe." And with a quick wave to Jack, he mounted star and quickly left the military depot in Ballston.

States saw a man coming up the road from the west. The snow was swirling around and the winter sun was near setting. "Who would be out on an evening like this?" he thought. Then he realized there was something familiar about that horse. "It's Star!" he shouted to his son, Isaac, who had been helping with the chores. "That must be Jim on Star!"

"Hello!" He shouted into the wind.

"Hello!" Jim shouted back as he gave Star a gentle nudge in the ribs. The horse picked up his gate as he also recognized his old home.

Young Isaac ran to the barn and flung open the door. "Put him in here, Jim!" he said in an excited voice.

"Can a tired soldier beg a meal and a warm bed?" Jim asked States as he slid off his horse.

"You sure can," States said, as he gave his cousin a warm hug. "Isaac, take Star into the barn. Pull his saddle off and give him some hay. Jim, come into the house and warm yourself up. The evening is getting quite cold."

"So, you were the first to see Jim when he came home?" Bobby asked States.

"Yes. Well, it was another half day ride up to Jewel Corner where Hannah and her family lived. It was a cold January night so Jim decided to stay with us and ride up in the morning," States explained. "We stayed up quite late that night while he told us of his adventures. The next day he continued home to his family."

Jim and Betsey were sitting in her father's parlor quietly when he felt the need to talk. Not of the war or of the battles, but of the children. First, he told of the burning of Newbury, Canada.

"I didn't think I would ever see a more heart-wrenching site than those Canadian women with their babies and children trying to keep warm that day," he told Betsey. "That was until we retreated from Buffalo a few days later. The road was full of homeless people fleeing east away from the savage Indians who would not hesitate to end their cold and misery. The lines went on for over fifty miles. It was pitiful. People, mostly women and children, stumbling along in the snow. We could do nothing for them. We just had to ride by."[96]

"When did man become so evil?" he went on. "The soldiering I can live with, but the evil actions against the women and children is very hard to take."

Betsey could see the war was changing him, not making him harder as it did some, but somehow softer. The confident soldier, sure of his job, was changing and more questioning. She put her arms around him as if to comfort him. He had grown up in that nine months. She could still see the soldier. He had not lost his personal confidence. It was the mission of the soldier that he was questioning. She loved this young man and quietly hoped he loved her also?

Chapter 15 - Napoleon Surrenders

"What think you of those changes in Europe that have so recently astonished the world, what effect will they have on our government and our citizens, shall we be overwhelmed with the present disposable force of Old England, will her fleets swarm on our coasts and our sacred soil groan beneath her legions?"

Capt. John W. Weeks. 11th Regt. Headquarters. Camp Buffalo: Letter to Samuel A. Pearson, Esq. June 28, year 1814. [97]

States was already seated on the veranda when Bobby arrived.

"Sorry, I'm late!" Bobby panted as he hurried to his usual chair.

"It's fine. You just gave me time to enjoy my coffee in peace," States answered. "Where do you want to start today?"

Taking a quick sip of the coffee that the girl brought over to him, Bobby paused for a moment, and answered, "Yesterday you had mentioned something about Napoleon. What did that have to do with our war with England?"

"You did say that you were not really up on your history, I guess," States answered. "Well, Napoleon, you do know who he is?"

"Yes!" Bobby answered. "The Frenchman."

"Yes, the Frenchman," States repeated, not trying to conceal his smile. "Well, the Frenchman surrendered to the British and abdicated his throne on April 6, 1814. This meant thousands of experienced British veteran soldiers would be free to get on the recently unneeded ships and sail to North America and fight here." [98]

"Oh! Of course," Bobby replied, realizing how little thought he had put into his last question.

States continued, "Well, by the end of June everyone in the military was wondering just what Napoleon's surrender might mean in our country's struggle against Britain."

"Jim and Betsey were no different than anyone else, and they took action on their ideas. Jim had moved into the little house at Tolls Mill. This meant that he would be closer to Betsey and her family at Stillwater," States concluded.

July14th, 1814

" . . . I'm sure I will have to go back in the militia soon," Jim had just finished saying. Betsey's little mare was quietly walking along side of Star on the road just south of Moons Resort and heading for Stillwater.

Betsey pulled her up short and stopped, "You have already been in almost a year. Why would you have to go?"

"Haven't you heard? Napoleon signed the 'Treaty of Fountain' and abdicated the throne in France. Their war is over now and all those British troops will be free to just come over here and invade us. We will surely have to defend Sackett's Harbor and Lake Champlain. Thousands of British soldiers will soon be gathering to come south and teach us a lesson. They know how divided we are," Jim explained. "All the soldiers have been talking about this for the last few days."

Betsey started to cry. She realized what this would mean. Jim and her brothers would surely be called again and they might well lose the battles. It had been too close when they were fighting mostly the Canadians.

She wanted to marry Jim and have a family. If what he said was right they could be called up any day. Jim was still active in the militia cavalry. They could be ready in a few days.

Jim pulled into a path that ran over to the lakeshore and dismounted. He helped Betsey off her horse and they sat in the sand. She was very quiet and he needed to know what was on her mind. When she did speak he was taken aback, but happy.

"Let's get married!" she said.

They had talked of marriage but Jim always thought they would have family around and a nice party. "Now?" he asked.

"Yes, right now! Today," she answered. She didn't want to lose him to the army or anyone else. "I know where the Justice of the Peace lives. It's not too far from here. We could start our honeymoon today," she said and smiled coyly at him. [99]

It made as much sense as anything in these crazy times. Ever since that wild escape from Fort Niagara on Star, he had wondered if his life might be cut short, even before he had lived. He had seen it happen to many young men already.

"Yes, let's do it," he heard himself say. He grabbed her and gave her a big kiss right there on the beach . . .

"Not so quick. We're not married yet!" she laughed.

Shortly after noon on July 14, 1814, the old justice of the peace had performed the simple ceremony. After the celebration they rode home to their folks at Jewel Corner and told them the news.

"In less than two months what everyone had dreaded came true," States explained. "On August 24, 1814, the British force of four-thousand men had attacked and burned the Capital at Washington DC."

"Two weeks later, on September thirteenth, Jim's unit was called up and sent to defend against the expected attack on Sackett's Harbor. It was on the same day that Francis Scott Key wrote the song, "The Star Spangled Banner," during the attack on Baltimore."[100]

"So as soon as Napoleon surrendered, the British turned their soldiers on us," Bobby stated. "I hadn't thought of the connection before. The War of 1812 was started by the British contention with Napoleon. When it was over, it would make it much easier for the British to defeat us."

"Well, sort of. Yes," States answered, "but it wasn't going to be that easy. Yes. No one was willing to defend Washington, but the militia and Governors did defend Baltimore, New York and the New York frontier at Plattsburg on Lake Champlain. And Jackson did defeat them at New Orleans, even if it was after the war ended. It had taken about two years but a few politicians and active young officers did learn how to defend our shores."

"Even President Madison realized we needed a federal standing army. If he didn't learn it from the British, his wife, Dolly, surely would have told him, because she had to flee Washington as they were coming in to attack."

"How did it all end then?" Bobby asked.

"There was one sad event yet to happen," States continued.

Jack and Sam O'Bryan were both part of the cavalry. [101] This year Sam was eighteen and his father said he could also join the Albany Volunteers Cavalry Unit. They had all signed on for three months. Since it was summer and time was essential they had been called as cavalry. The trip up to

Sackett's Harbor took six days on horseback. The roads were still in very poor condition from Little Falls north to the Harbor, but they still were able to make good time. "I believe they must have traveled thirty-five miles a day," Jack thought.

Jim was quite excited when he rode into Sackett's Harbor. The reason for his excitement was simple. Even though his father had come home a few months earlier, his cousin, Buddy, with the 13th US Infantry was now stationed there. [102] He had not seen him since he had signed up.

The little village was full of soldiers. Tents and men were everywhere. Jim's unit was put into tents by the Volunteer Fort because of a lack of more substantial quarters. The Silver Grays Company had been discharged when the 13th US Infantry came in with General Wilkinson's Brigade.

"Sergeant, do you happen to know where the 13th Infantry is quartered?" Jim asked.

"I believe they are in the barracks by Fort Tompkins," he replied.

"Would it be alright if I took an hour and went over to look up my cousin," Jim went on.

"That would be okay. See if they have any news we may have missed on our trip up here," the Sergeant requested.

"Sure," Jim volunteered, as he started west toward Fort Tompkins.

Buddy was just finishing his evening meal when Jim finally discovered him. He looked older than his thirty-four years. Thinner, and maybe in some ways, harder.

"Buddy! How are you doing?" Jim greeted him.
Buddy's head lifted up when he heard his old familiar nickname. Everyone in the 13th had called him, 'George.'

"Jim! When did you get here?" Buddy exclaimed with a big smile across his face.

"Just this evening," Jim answered, as he grasped his cousin's hand.

The young men sat down and brought each other up-to-date on their latest news, and Jim told of his wedding and the latest news from his family. Buddy wanted to know how Mary and his family were doing and, once he was assured everything was well at home, he quickly turned to tell of his recent actions in Canada.

Buddy mostly talked about Secretary Armstrong and General Wilkinson's misadventure downriver to Montreal the fall before. And he continued to describe the battle at Chrysler's farm and the wintering over in the Plattsburg area on Lake Champlain. Buddy had told Jim what everyone was already beginning to realize.

"The Secretary of War, Armstrong, is very incompetent," he began. "Old General Wilkinson is even worse. Neither understands how to keep their army supplied. So, by spring, thousands were sick and dying of typhoid and other diseases.

"We had to leave a large contingent at Plattsburg when we moved back to Sackett's Harbor because they were so sick," he went on. "Now, here, there are not enough barracks and still no new ones are being built. The camp hospital is overflowing with the sick and disabled. We don't need to fight to lose our men. We lose a few more every day. [103]

"We were in good shape after the battle of Crysler's Farm, but we were so short on supplies with no hope of getting any. So old Wilkinson just walked over to the river and crossed back to our side of the river. It had all been done for nothing.

"In confidence, Captain Kearney told a bunch of us when it was over. There never was a chance of taking Montreal. It was just old Armstrong's glorious vision of being the man who would conquer Canada. The younger officers all knew that when they didn't have enough men to take the shipbuilding port of Kingston, it would all be a meaningless adventure. A lot of good men were killed because of one old man's pipedream. Now with Napoleon's surrender, it would definitely be a defensive war."

Jim sat quietly as his older cousin poured out his feelings of bitterness, disgust and trepidation. He realized how important the commanders were. He was also very thankful, having served under General Brown in 1813.

"Well, we have enough men to defend this location if they come back again," Jim told his cousin.

"There will be an invasion, that's for sure. I just don't think they know where it will be," Buddy continued. Jim could sense Buddy was not his old self. The confidence seemed to be gone.

"Well, I better get back. I'll look you up when I can," he said as he got up to leave. "We will be in and out. The word is out that we will be patrolling from the fort west to Henderson's Point."

Jim visited his cousin a few more times, and the last time he stopped by, he was told that Buddy had come down with Camp Fever, typhoid, and was in the hospital.

States then finished his story. "The attack never came. Instead it was at Plattsburg. The defenses held and old Sir Prevost returned to Canada. Jim was discharged on December 12, 1814, and given eight days to travel home. A number of those from the 13th were so sick they were discharged and had been sent home also. Buddy was one of them, but sadly, he never made it home. He died of the fever on the way, in mid-December of that year."[104] States swallowed hard as he remembered how the sadness had settled over the whole family.

"Buddy never saw his wife or children again. How sad!" Bobby commented.

"No! He never made it home . . . just another one of New York's young men who died on that cold Canadian border . . . in a war almost no one knows or cares about," States answered. "Buddy's wife, Mary, never remarried. She raised her seven children by herself with the help of George and Hannah, much as my mother had done."

"That's about it for the War of 1812. George and his friends in the Silver Grays Company were perhaps the only ones who really understood what was at stake. Mostly, it was the lives of their sons and the vague concept of freedom. The politicians had finally learned they needed an army, but it had come too late for the new Capital city of Washington and thousands of young men like Buddy."

"Do you have enough for your article?" States said as he stood up to go home.

Bobby thought for a moment. "Maybe one more session," he said. "I have a lot of loose ends. Did old George die at Jewel Corner? And what happened to Jim and Harmon's families on the Free Farm? Did they lose it to the bigwigs?" [105]

"Okay, one more session," States replied. "Make sure your questions are clear. I would like to see these interviews finished before I die."

Bobby caught the hint of a smile on the old man's face. This had become a story of one family and what they had done for the last eighty or so years. He would need to wrap up the story of the family in his article. "Goodbye, States. So I will see you tomorrow then?" Bobby asked.

"Yes, tomorrow then," States replied, as he shuffled away.

Chapter 16 - The Year With No Summer

In May 1816, frost killed off most of the crops that had been planted, and on June 4th, 1816, frosts were reported in Connecticut, and by the following day, most of New England was gripped by the cold front. On June 6th, 1816, snow fell in Albany, New York, and in Dennysville, Maine; nearly a foot of snow was observed in Quebec City in early June, with consequent additional loss of crops. The result was regional malnutrition, starvation, epidemic, and increased mortality. [106]

"Darkness"
By Lord Byron

"I had a dream, which was not all a dream.
The bright sun was extinguished, and the stars
Did wander darkling in the eternal space,
Rayless, and pathless, and the icy earth
Swung blind and blackening in the moonless air;
Morn came and went... and came, and brought no day,
And men forgot their passions in the dread
Of this their desolation; and all hearts
Were chilled into a selfish prayer for light." [107]

Bobby was seated on the veranda when the old man arrived. He had his questions before him and thought this session might be a quick one. States also sat down and the server brought him his coffee and a hot sweet.

"So, you want to wrap up the loose ends to our family story," States began. "I was thinking about that and realized it might take a while. Things had begun to get bad for the Jewels in 1815. [108]Jesse Toll sold his mills to Mr. Granger and they were shut down to be rebuilt. This alone was not the problem."

"For us, the loss of Jewel Bridge was the most difficult. George had to sell it when Jesse shut down his mill. There were not enough tolls to make the collection worthwhile. The youngest boys took the lost the hardest. Jim and Tom were part of the bridge and it was part of them. Hannah also loved this bridge that her husband had made. She was proud that the little community, only a few houses, was going to be called Jewel Bridge."

"It was, for her, a personal thing. George and Hannah had basically lived at Jewel Corner since their son, William, had died in 1808. However, the bridge and the old house always made it still feel like home somehow. Jim and Tom still used the old house whenever they worked around Saratoga Springs."

"Things continued to get worse. Did you ever hear about the year with no summer?" States asked.

"No! When was that?" Bobby answered.

"Basically it was 1816. Now we realize it started with the eruption of a volcano somewhere on the other side of the world in April of 1815.[109] But then, no one knew what was happening. Many thought God had abandoned them. During the fall of 1815 the skies were very red. Then the winter of 1815 and '16 came on extremely bitter and cold," States explained.

"During the spring of 1816 the snow was very slow in melting. And for reasons no one knew at the time, it froze every month of the summer. Most of the crops failed and thousands starved to death in New England and northern New York State."

. . . but by November of 1816, Susannah had heard that Abraham Jewel, one of George and Hannah's older boys, was back home and down on the lake fishing almost every day. It was a long cold ride from Jewel Corner down to the lake and she was concerned for Hannah and her family.

"States, would you ride over to the lake and see if Abraham Jewel is there? If so, bring him here so he can warm up and have a good meal. So many are hungry these days."

"Sure, Mother," States replied politely. "I think I know where he will be fishing. He will probably be spearing on the edge of the reeds where Fish Creek leaves the lake. When we were younger we all called that our special place."

States put on his warmest riding coat and then rode over to Saratoga Lake. The ice had long been frozen thick enough to ride on. As he approached the Lake's outlet, he could see a small black speck in the distance. The blowing snow was especially cold on his face. As he approached the man he shouted out, "Abraham!" not sure who he was talking to.

"Yah!" his cousin answered.

"It is you!" States went on. "How long have you been home?"

"About a month. I've decided to come home and help Ma and Pa," Abe answered.

"My mother wants you to come up and have dinner with us. She is concerned about Aunt Hannah and her family," States continued.

"I just as well. I haven't seen a fish in hours," Abe replied. "My horse is tied over there in the woods. Let me get him and I will go up with you."

Back at his home, States shouted through the door, "Abe is here!"

Susannah was full of questions for her nephew. However, the answers to most of them were depressing.

"Things are quite desperate over at Jewel Corner," Abe said. "The reason I am coming down here to fish is that most of the local game and fish at Gansevoort has all been taken by so many hungry people."

Abe explained, "With no good hay the cow's milk had dried up. The gardens all failed. All they had were wild foods with fish and squirrels to flavor the soups. Pa and Ma sent Jim and Betsey over to the Free Farm on the Sacandaga to help Isaac hunt and fish to feed his little ones. Pa thought there would be more game over there because there were fewer people."

"You will stay the night and tomorrow we will take the sleigh up. I need to see my sister," Susannah ordered.

Abe didn't argue. He was too weak himself and States could see also, that he was not well.

When the sleigh pulled into George and Hannah's home, it was loaded with some potatoes, onions and hams. When Susannah saw Hannah, she thought that she looked far beyond her sixty-six years. Her eyes were sunken and it was obvious she had not been eating, giving most of the food to Mary's children.

"Hannah, why didn't you say something?" Susannah asked, as the tears came to her eyes.

Hannah smiled with a weak smile. "It's okay, sister. I've had a good life. I'm ready and I'm tired. My boys are grown and no longer need me. Thank you for the food. Mary's Maria is strong and she will use it to feed the young ones."

They talked of old times and Susannah could see a peaceful smile come over her sister's face. But she knew her light would soon go out. George was hunting as he did every day, a rabbit here and a squirrel there. Their short visit was necessary to avoid a trip home in the darkness.

States could hear his mother crying quietly as they started for home. He also knew that his own live would change after this miserable winter.

States then summarized for Bobby. "The help came way too late. By spring Hannah and Abe were both gone, taken by that awful disease, the consumption."[110]

Then States continued on, "In 1818 George and Jim sold the mill to Mathew Ketchum and moved west to the military tracts. They located themselves and families in the town of Cato in Cayuga County.[111] They took Mary and her children with them. The only Jewel boys left in Saratoga County were Tom and Harmon's second boy, Joe.

"Tom had moved back to Saratoga as a blacksmith. He started a blacksmith shop next to the old house in Grangerville, which is what we call the community by Jesse Toll's mill pond.

"Joe was still on his half of the Free Farm in Edinburgh. They lost the water rights but the rich bottomland Indian field along the Sacandaga grew beautiful corn and wheat. He also found employment in the local timber industry as a carpenter."

Chapter 17 - Banks and the Erie Canal

1816 - The approval of (Hamilton's Federalists) Second National Bank of the United States – Madison, a Jeffersonian, realized a national army was needed. He went on to endorse the tariff of 1816, to provide the money to pay for it. – The war of 1812 had more or less destroyed the Federalist Party but Madison's acceptance of so much of the policies made the point mute and a period of good feelings began in 1820 – Monroe yielded more ground. State Banks expanded in the west and money became plentiful. [112]

1816 – The Erie Canal Project started up again. John Richardson started building the Erie Canal. (probably with the expansion of Rensselear's NY State Bank)

. . . States continued with his story.

"Well, Hannah's death became a passage of sorts for Uncle George. He thought less about how he needed to help his family. Instead, he focused on the changes going around in our new country. I used to tease him about becoming a philosopher of sorts . . . 'Whatever that is,' he would quip back."

"A second big problem after the war was the money. Some wanted paper money and others wanted only gold and silver coins. The big bank was the National Bank. Its charter was passed by Congress and signed by Madison in 1816. There also were state banks. State banks could also print money, but the National Bank legislation required them to keep a specific reserve.

The Jewel family boys were also trying to understand what all the fuss was about concerning paper money.

"How does that work, Uncle George?" Joe asked. "How can Mr. Rensselear's bank just print money, sign it and then use it to hire me to dig the canal?"

"I'm not sure," George answered. "I guess he is so rich that if anyone takes one of his bills into the bank and asks for gold he would just give it to them. People trust him, I guess. But I know one thing, it doesn't always work."

"What do you mean, Uncle George?" Joe asked. "The government printed money during the war, and soon it became worthless and no one would take it. The older people, like me, remember those bad times. They called it 'runaway inflation.' We had to use the barter system. That's where you trade work for things. People just wouldn't accept the worthless money," George answered.

Then he continued, "Now, when you work on the Erie Canal project, the foreman pays you in Mr. Rensselear's bank notes. You can buy food or a new horse with them. As long as they can buy what you need and don't get worthless each year, the system works."

"But if I take a Rensselear note to Virginia it may not be worth as much, you are saying?" Joe asked.

"That's true if you want to take the money to some other state. You better get one of Mr. Biddle's dollars from the National Bank or, better yet, have a gold coin," George replied.

"So, if there was no gold and I did some work for someone, how could they pay me without paper money?" Joe asked.

"That's the problem," George said. "There is a breakdown of trade if there isn't money that can be trusted to pay each other. That's why, on the Free Farm, they want us to pay our rent with wheat."

"That's also why Hamilton wanted the rich people to run the banks and government. He knew trade didn't work without money, or currency, as he called it. When he was a very young man, he ran a trading house for an old man down in the Caribbean. He learned that money is simply another word for trust. It's like, if I work for my neighbor and he gives me an "I owe you" for five dollars, it's his money. If I come back in the fall with the 'I-Owe-You' and give it back, he will give me five dollars' worth of his wheat. If I can't trust him, I won't work for his 'I Owe You.' In simple terms, money is like the grease that keeps trade going."

"So, all this talk of paper money or gold and silver is not important if we trust the banks," Joe summarized.

"That's right, but can we trust the banks, or better yet, the bankers? That's the question," George said with a big smile on his face.

"You know how the price of land has been going up these days?" George continued.

"Yes," Joe answered.

"Well, that is because all the people working on the canal have Mr. Rensselear's dollars. These dollars are so plentiful that people are willing to give more of them for the land. That's the risk with paper money. If there is too much of it, it loses its value. But if there is too little no one can find a job," George explained.

"But if I borrow money and buy land and the land gets worth more, then I can sell the land and keep the extra money," Joe stated.

"Yes, but if you buy land with timber on it and the president makes a new law like President Jefferson did in 1807, then you can't sell the timber and you have no money to pay off your note. Then the note-holder gets your land. But for now, as the price of land goes up, it might be okay to buy some land. But it will be best if you just buy what you can afford without borrowing too much money," George suggested.

States asked Bobby, "Do you understand about money and speculation?"

"Sure," Bobby agreed. "Buy low and sell high!" Then he laughed.

"Yes," States said, "but how do you do that, Bobby? That is the question."

Bobby shifted in his seat and weakly admitted, "States, I really don't know."

"Well," States began, "Joe and his friend, James Partridge, were serious about how this paper money and these mortgage notes worked. Uncle George was going west, over to Cato, and he would not be available to ask for advice. Joe respected his uncle's knowledge, but their little school never told him about the problems of paper money and he wanted to know. He was eighteen-years old and ready to be on his own. So, now with the construction of the Erie Canal, money was plentiful and land prices were going up. And Joe wanted to become a speculator."

"So, I'm thinking the Erie Canal provided the money and jobs to make life better for their communities," Bobby added.

"That's about it. Almost everyone was speculating in something. Joe knew timber very well. And James Partridge's father was wondering if the boys wanted to buy land, cut the timber off and then sell it. None of the Jewel boys were timid," States continued. "Joe knew his half of the leased Free Farm was not worth much, so he was looking to get a stake so he could marry his girl, Hannah Greenfield, in Edinburgh."

"One other important thing was going on at that time," States said, changing the subject. "Remember how I said most men could not vote on what we now call the Upper House or the New York State Senate. And this Senate appointed the sheriffs and judges that ran the courts. In fact, the wealthy, one time federalists and bigwigs still did pretty much whatever they wanted to do. Well the old soldiers, the "Silver Grays," and a bunch of their sons, like Jim, would no longer accept this. They needed to own land to have the right to vote. So they abandoned the manors in Duchess and Albany Counties. They left their leased farms and moved onto the Indian lands in the west which were owned by old soldiers and speculators. On these lands they could get warranty titles and actually own the land. This increased the number of so called 'Free Holder,' voters, and they became the majority."

"However, the factory workers were still very poor and could not vote. This new majority of small farm owners forced the New York government to revise its State Constitution in 1821 and remove the landholding requirement for voters on the Upper House. [113]They also changed many of the formerly appointed offices to be voted on in local elections. This change increased the voting base from two in five to five in five. Six years later, these new voters, including the millworkers, made slavery illegal in New York. This allowed them to secure higher wages since slave labor was no longer available. The cast was finally set to begin to destroy the feudalism in New York."

"This brought a time of expansion and prosperity to thousands of families formally held down by the tentacles of feudalism. These tentacles still existed in Albany and Dutchess

Counties, but the tenants and labors voted with their feet and moved West," States continued.

"What you are saying then is this," Bobby summarized. "It was not the Revolution that brought freedom to Colonial New York and changed it into a real State. That didn't happen until 1821, and it was done by a bunch of old Revolutionary War soldiers and their sons. These men had to again defend New York from the British and would no longer accept lives of servitude."

"That about it," States answered. "Without those internal battles by old soldiers like George and his son Jim, Alexander Hamilton and his bigwig friends like, Livingstone, Schuyler and Rensselear would still be running New York. It would still be like an English feudal kingdom with the governor as king. Did you ever hear that Hamilton originally wanted the President and the Senate to be elected for life terms?"

"No!" Bobby answered. "Really!"

"Yes! He did," States replied. "History doesn't always record the sordid details of men they want to turn into heroes.

"In 1818 Uncle George, his son Jim, his nephew Harmon and his son, James B, Joe's older brother, were all part of this change. They picked up their families and moved to the town of Cato, in Cayuga County, here in New York. They were joined by some of the Jewels from Fishkill over in Dutchess County. This new area was part of the former Cayuga Indian lands that had been handed out to the old Revolutionary War soldiers. The awards were generous. Privates got five to six hundred acres depending on how long they served. The officers got thousands of acres. A colonel would often get five thousand acres." [114]

"George's old Colonel, Samuel Drake, went to Cayuga County. He got a good award. His Captain Ladue also got many acres. They sold this land cheap right after the war when George and Jim went out and bought their land by "Weeds

Basin." Now we call it 'Weeds Port.' Their farm was right along the Seneca River and, as usual, it had a nice small stream that could be dammed up to run a little mill."

"How cheap was cheap?" Bobby asked.

"Well some of the soldiers never planned to go west. They sold it often for less than a dollar per acre. But good farms were about two to four dollars per acre if my memory serves me right," States answered.

They didn't go out alone. George's son, Daniel, and his wife, Rachel's people, the Churches, came with him. George's cousin, Isaac DeLameter, and his son, Samuel, also were in the neighborhood. In fact, George's daughter, Hannah, married Samuel."

The four Jewel farms at Weedsport NY, 1850's

"These Jewel families all had children. Jim had twelve. There was also Joe's older brother, James B. Buddy and Mary's oldest daughter, Marie, married a boy named Robert Gault. George would just say, 'the young ones are all doing well.'"

"Well, what happened to Joe and Tom, the young men that didn't go west?" Bobby asked.

141

"Well, I was getting to that," States answered. "Like I said, there was a lot of money around. The Erie Canal was finished about 1825."

"Joe and James Partridge took up old Mr. Partridge's offer and started woods walking for timber. The logs were used for the wood tool industry that grew up around the waterpower site. It was that same power site from the old Free Farm but the Manor Lord, Rensselear, sold it to a man named Cook. Joe just had to adjust. He still farmed the good bottomland along the Sacandaga River but he worked in the wood tool industry also."

"So, the old Bigwig Manor Lord, Rensselear, did cheat them out of the waterpower site as they expected?" Bobby inquired.

"Yes, that was clear when George decided to move west in 1818," States stated. "But he told his sons to stay positive and work with what they had. So they had a nice home, good bottomland fields, plenty of industry to work for and a beautiful river to fish in with their boys."

"Joe took to his woods walking like a duck takes to water. He soon had enough money to marry Hannah Greenfield, his sweetheart. Her brothers, the Greenfield boys were half Indian, as they say, and Joe fit right in. But instead of furs and venison, he focused on pine and oak timber."

"So was he speculating in timber or land then?" Bobby asked.

"Well, you could say both or you could say neither," States said with a big grin.

"That's no answer," Bobby teased back.

"What I mean, is this," States continued. "Joe wasn't speculating on the timber or the land. He knew both but he was speculating on the market. In 1832 he could see that was changing, so he sold over two-hundred acres of his family's investments. His father, Harmon, and his older brother, James

142

B, wanted to move into the Michigan frontier, so it was the ideal time to sell. It was all connected to that banking question that he had asked his uncle about years earlier, and the new President Andrew Jackson's fight with a man named Biddle . . ."

Joe's Free Farm in Edinburgh

Chapter 18 - Jackson (vs) Biddle

. . . 1824, and again in 1828, Andrew Jackson (an old soldier himself) was elected President. His views were in direct opposite to Alexander Hamilton's economic system as the following quote makes clear:

"I am one of those who do not believe that a national debt is a national blessing," **he said,** *"but rather a curse to a republic; inasmuch as it is calculated to raise around the administration a moneyed aristocracy dangerous to the liberties of the country."*

Biddle's National Bank was due to have its charter expire in 1836. Jackson set himself a goal to destroy the National Bank. He felt it made Biddle, an unelected private aristocrat, much too powerful.

The problem with Biddle's bank was, "It could issue bank notes up to the physical ability of the president and cashier to sign them; after 1827 it evaded this limitation by the invention of 'branch drafts' which looked and circulated like notes but were actually bills of exchange." [115]

. . . Then States began, "Jackson believed the Hamiltonian economic system was pure evil, and that was best understood in Biddle's National Bank. He summed up the problem like this:"

"The planter, the farmer, the mechanic and the labor," **he wrote.** *All know that their success depends upon their own industry and economy, and that they must not expect to become suddenly rich by the fruits*

144

of their toil; these classes form the great body of the people of the United States; they are the bone and sinew of the country. "Yet," they are in constant danger of losing fair influence in Government. "Why"? The mischief springs from the power which the moneyed interests derive from a paper currency, which they are able to control, from the multitude of corporations with exclusive privileges which they have succeeded in obtaining in the different states." His warning to his people was solemn. "Unless you become more watchful . . . you will in the end find that the most important powers of government will have been given or bartered away, and the control over your dearest interests has passed into the hands of these corporations." [116]

States finished his coffee after lunch and posed a question to Bobby, "Did you ever hear about President Jackson's 'Hard Money/Paper Money' controversy?"

"No, I can't say that I have," the young man confessed.

States asked, "Did you ever read a book by William M. Gouge called, "*A Short History of Paper Money and Banking in the United States?*"

"Doesn't sound like anything I would be interested in," Bobby confessed, wondering why this old man wanted to talk about banking.

"Well, in the 1830s everyone was interested in it. State banks were printing money as fast as they could. Fortunes were being made by bankers and speculators every day. Land prices were rising so fast that the poor people were being shut out of the prosperity," States replied.

"Joe wasn't rich but he was speculating, wasn't he?" Bobby asked.

"Yes, that was what I was getting to. My son, Isaac, also bought a big farm, thinking he would also get in on the boom," States answered, "but Joe had read Mr. Gouge's book. So he sold his investments in 1832, knowing it all would soon end."

"To fight the wealthy bankers, President Jackson did two things. First, he stopped putting government tax money in Biddle's National bank, and instead, put it in several of the existing state banks. This caused a flurry of new business enterprises, making the problem worse. Then he stopped accepting state banks' paper money for the payment of federal land and then required gold. No one had enough gold so land sales stopped and prices fell. I had to buy my son's property to salvage his investments when the crash finally came in 1837."

States explained, "Mr. Gouge's book had written aout the problem something like this:

"Some called them self-generating business cycles. Banks incline to over issue their notes. Prices then rise and a speculative fever begins to spread. Excited by the appearance of prosperity that accompanies a boom, people spend freely. The general expansion of credit leads to over trading and inflation. Every new business operation on credit creates more promissory notes and these increase the demand for discounts, till finally, the currency depreciates so greatly that 'specie' (gold and silver coins) is required for export in order to pay foreign debts. With specie at a premium, contraction sets in. Banks call in their loans, timid people starts runs on banks, contraction turns to panic and panic to collapse. 'One man is unable to pay his debts,' wrote Gouge. His creditor depended on him for the means of paying a third person to whom he himself is indebted. The circle extends through society. Multitudes go bankrupt and a few successful speculators get possession of the earnings and savings of many of their frugal and industrious neighbors." [117]

"Well, who was right then, Hamilton's bankers or Jefferson and Jackson's hard money policy?" Bobby asked again.

"Well, it's like Uncle George said earlier, 'it's not who's right but what's right,'" States answered. "Greedy bankers or land speculators who expect to become rich without effort are wrong. People who suck the value out of trade without putting anything in are wrong. It's only right when the prosperity is shared fairly and it is tied to a legitimate personnel effort."

"Joe had followed Uncle George's advice. He had not bought a lot or more land than he could afford. His knowledge and skill as a woods walker meant that he knew he was buying valuable timber. And he was providing an actual service when he delivered the timber to the wood industry along the Sacandaga. He was also careful not to be too greedy. He got out before the 1837 collapse because he knew it was all built on speculation and not real work."

George's Last Mill

Bobby asked States, "I just need a few more items. I need to wrap up what happened to old George. And what did Jim do out west?"

"Well, in 1818, old George was only seventy-eight years old. He died at one-hundred and three so he lived twenty-five years longer."

"To really explain the struggle that the old soldiers and their sons had, we need to talk about their continuing fight against New York's feudal system."

Chapter 19 - The Free Farm

Stephen van Rensselaer, with the assistance of Alexander Hamilton, created a "durable lease" that would bind his tenants and their heirs to the manor in perpetuity. By calling the contract an "incomplete sale," Hamilton had devised a means to sidestep the issue of feudalism, which had been outlawed in New York State in 1787. Tenants were required to pay the patroon an annual rent of ten to twenty bushels of winter wheat per one hundred acres, "four fat fowl," and a day's labor with a team of horses and wagon. In addition, the tenant was to pay all taxes and use the land for agricultural purposes only, while the patroon kept all timber, mineral, and water rights, as well as the right to exploit those resources. These leases also provided that when a tenant chose to sell all or part of his farm, was thus required to pay a "quarter sale" or one-fourth of the sale price to the patroon in order to release the property to another individual or party. Hence, the patroon kept all the advantages of land ownership, and the tenant had all of the obligations of land improvement, road building and taxes. This was not quite the binding to the land of the old European feudal system, but it was fairly close in actual effect. [118]

States began, "Originally, like I said, handbills were distributed announcing that the patroon would give the patriots of the Revolution homesteads without cost. The conditions of the grants stated that a farmer selects a one-hundred and twenty acre farm location. Then he clears it, builds a dwelling, and lives there free for seven years. At the end of this time, he would have to go to the manor office and receive a "durable lease" with a moderate annual rent to be paid in wheat. Like George, about three-thousand families took Van Rensselaer's offer. Many of these new tenants were 'Yankees' who had spread across New England and had begun to overflow into New York State." [119]

Bobby asked, "Did they just go out and squat on land anywhere?"

"No," States answered. "Jacob Winne and John Preston, local surveyors, were hired to mark off many of the West Manor lots. The task of surveying manor lands was largely completed by 1795 and was documented in field books and maps that included detailed information about the physical characteristics of the land."

"Like I said earlier, Bobby, when George went down to help build the bridge at the Fish House, along the Sacandaga, he selected a property for his son, Isaac, and his cousin, Harmon. It was about 1800. Both men was newly married."

"During the difficult years, between 1808 and 1818, this home belonged to Isaac and Harmon. In 1818 they both moved west. Harmon's second son, Joe, stayed on the property. They lost the water rights but there was enough value for Joe and his family to survive quite well. There were a few rich bottomland fields along the river."

"George taught his family how to use the values that the river provided. They could always use it to provide fish and furs. It also allowed them to transport logs, lumber and other commerce. The Jewel boys were experts in boating, rafting and moving the wood products on the water. The mountain lands upstream were still full of logs and other products. Joe's new in-laws, the Greenfields, were still heavily involved in hunting, fishing and trapping."

"So the Free Farm was not such a bad deal after all?" Bobby interrupted.

"It was not so much that the Free Farm was such a good deal. It was much more connected to what kind of men George had taught his family to be. George always taught them the very usable skills needed to survive in the wilderness. Their skills were honed to change the wilderness into a livable community. In a sense they were builders."

"In the end there was not much value realized from the manor lords' properties. When Tom and Joe moved west they sold their properties very cheap. In 1846 Tom sold the old home in Grangerville for twenty-five dollars, and Joe sold his sixty-acre half of the Free Farm for one-hundred and fifty dollars, less than three dollars per acre. They also voted with their feet and moved to Wisconsin." [120]

Chapter 20 - Death of the Old Soldier

Have you seen the Sacandaga,
where it rises in the mountains,
in its Adirondack fountains?

Where forests bend and listen,
to the answering echoes singing?
Where wildflowers lightly bending,
smile to see the never-ending?

Yes, we have seen the Sacandaga
and have heard the gurgling fountains;
Seen the beautiful Sacandaga
winding through the glorious mountains.

There with all thy wealth of flowers;
there within thy heavenly bowers.
Oh, to pitch a tent again;
oh to drift in dreams eternal [121]

"Well, whatever happened to old George?" Bobby asked.

"I guess I should finish this," States added. "He lived with his family along the Seneca River near Weeds Port. Most of the time he was telling stories to the children or going down by the river to fish and talk to the Erie Canal boatmen. Sometimes he would listen for jobs that his boys might do to supplement their farming income.

One cold morning in 1843 in Edinburgh

d to stop by the post office and pick up a letter. "Who do you suppose it will be from Pa?" his son asked as he ran alongside of his father's great stride.

"I don't know. We will just have to wait a few minutes to find out," Pa said as he smiled down at his five-year old son. Joe also wondered who the letter might be from as they entered the little post office. The letter laid in a box that was marked with the name 'Jewel.'

"It's from my cousin's daughter, Marie," he told his son and opened the letter and read it quietly to himself.

> Dear Joe,
>
> "Sissy's husband is quite sick and she feels she can no longer take care of her father. My husband says I can only take him for a short while. He helped him apply for a pension under the Revolutionary War Pension Act of 1832, but it has been rejected. Your old cousin, George, wanted me to ask if he could go home to your place in Edinburgh which he loved so much."
>
> "Let me know if you can work something out."
>
> Love, Marie

"What does it say, Pa?" the boy asked, after what seemed a very long time to him.

"Marie says your old cousin George wants to come and live with us," Joe explained, as he started to ponder the issue.

"Can he? Can he?" his son excitedly cried.

"I don't know. We will have to talk to your mother. But it was his house, you know. He and my father built it when I was just a little boy," Joe told his son.

Later when Joe spoke to his wife about the request he was relieved to hear her answer. "He gave us all we have. Of course, we need to pay rent but, if it wasn't for old George we would be much worse off. Sure, we can take him. I'm sure it will not be for too long. He is going to be one-hundred and three years old this year, isn't he?" his wife asked. She knew that Joe wanted to make old George comfortable the last little bit of his long life.

Joe knew that George never kept anything for himself. Tom lived in the house that he built in Grangeville. He helped all his boys to get started in the Cato area. It would be unthinkable not to make him comfortable in the last few months of his life.

As they rode the train out to Syracuse, Joe looked at his two oldest boys on the seat beside him. The oldest was seven and the youngest was five. It was the proper thing that they should get acquainted with their father's old cousin. They both knew he rode as a Minute Man in the Revolutionary War, but they had only seen him once or twice.

When they arrived in Cato, George was glad to see them. The family was good to him but he could see that Old George was not comfortable at their place. The few things that he had could have easily been loaded on the train, but George had made his own arrangements to travel east on a riverboat. He was glad too, that Joe had brought the two boys. That way, they all could take his last canal boat ride together.

"It's alright, George. We can take a few days to get home," Joe said to his cousin.

153

"So, Old George went back to Saratoga County then?" Bobby asked States as he took a sip of coffee on the veranda.

"Yes, George always loved the little Free Farm along the Sacandaga in Edinburgh. It reminded him of his childhood along the Croton River over in Westchester County by Pine's Bridge," States continued. "He lived about a year along one of the rivers that he loved. He always said, 'Lakes are nice but rivers are always going somewhere.'"

"A short while later, in 1845, the old soldier died. George had nothing left to leave to anyone. He gave it all away during his lifetime."

"Joe had taken him back to the little old cemetery by Jewel Bridge to be buried with Hannah, William and Abraham, just a short distance from here. They are all buried there in the little community plot along Fish Creek."

"That's a great story. Whatever happed to Joe?" Bobby asked?

"Well, I got a letter from him a few years ago, about 1868. He lives on a nice farm near Green Bay, Wisconsin," States said.

"So, Bobby, you now have the story. George Washington, Thomas Jefferson, and Alexander Hamilton may have been our founding fathers, but the Jewel boys, their friends, and other 'Sons of Liberty' as well as the Silver Grays, always had to be there to keep the founding fathers on the true path of freedom."

With that, old States shut his eyes and Bobby thought he heard a gentle snore. He knew the interview was over. He quietly thanked the old man, still not sure what he would write, but he definitely had enough to make a story.

Bobby's notes: In 1782 the Revolution was over but the fight for freedom was just beginning. You have to meet an old soldier and his sons I know of . . . his name was George Jewel . . ."

Notes - For those who are interested

States Jewel died December 17th, 1875 at the age of 98. He is buried in a local cemetery of his beloved home city, Saratoga Springs, NY. His second wife Clarisse (Holmes) Jewel moved to Michigan after his death, where she live about two years and died at the age of 99.

States' mother, Susannah (Jewel) Ketchum, is buried in the little Jewel family cemetery on the north shore of Saratoga Lake, along Dyer Switch Road. A mother of the Revolution and a true Heroin of our Nation. States first wife and many of his family also reside in that little cemetery.

Old George Jewel, our hero, died about 1845, probably in Weeds Port. We don't know where he was buried. Most of the early Jewell cemeteries are very badly disintegrated. He may have been in the small cemetery by the school just north of his son's farms in Cato or as we tell in the story returned to Saratoga.

Hannah Jewell, George's wife, moved with the family to Saratoga, then to Jewel Corner. We are unsure what happened then. We believe she may have perished with her son Abraham in 1816. We found no burial site. That was marked. She is probably in one of the three Jewel Cemeteries in the Saratoga County Area.

James G. Jewel, (Jim) survived the War of 1812, sold his property in Saratoga and moved with his father to a farm across the Seneca River from Weed's Port, NY, He raised 12 children and died there on Feb. 15, 1860.

Young George Jewel, (Buddy) Died of typhoid fever in December, 1814, as outlined in the story. His wife Mary, never

156

remarried, She lived with her daughter some and her son some in the area of Weed's Port and then Springfield, Otsego, County, NY.

Young Hannah Jewel, (Sissy) Married Isaac Delamater's son, Samuel and lived next to her brother's farm in Weeds Port, NY.

Daniel Jewel live and died in 1838 a few miles to the north. He is buried in the Stone church cemetery. His wife, Lydia Church Jewel moved with her son in about 1838 to Michigan and lived a few miles north of the little village of Detroit.

Harmon Jewel, Joe's father and his son, Joe's brother, James B Jewel moved to Grand Rapids Michigan in 1833 and were among the first to establish there.

Joseph H. Jewel, (Joe) and his wife Hannah Greenfield Jewel, my great, great, grandfather moved to Geneva Wisconsin, with Isaac Jewel, presumable a relative, in 1846. Then they moved north to the big pine country of Hortonville, Wisconsin, where he died on March 30, 1878 and is buried there. Hannah moved with her son Leonard to Birch Cooley, Minnesota and died there on Feb. 17, 1890.

George Jewel and his sons were among the first on fish Creek, they built Jewel Bridge which took Burgoyne road over fish creek and eventually to Saratoga Springs, but as true to their calling they quickly moved west along the Erie Canal, building a new nation as they went. First too Western New York, then Michigan and Wisconsin.

Bibliography

Books:

Adams, Henry, 1838-1918, *The War of 1812*, Cooper Square Press, NY, NY, Edited, John R. Elting, 1999. A reprint of 1944 edition published in Washington DC. Which was excerpted from the nine volume edition of the, *History of The United states during the Administrations of Jefferson and Madison* (1889-1891). (Adams)

Bockee, Marie & Tower, Carpenter, Editors, *The Records of the Reformed Dutch Church of New Hackensack, Dutchess County New York* , Printed Poughkeepsie, New York ,1932, Heritage Book Inc.; Bowie MD Oct.1, 2007 (Hackensack Ch)

Bayard, Charles J. *"The development of public land policy 1783-1820,"* (p – 143, 144.) (Bayard,)

Bowers, Claude G., *Making Democracy a Reality, Jefferson, Jackson and Polk*, Memphis State College Press, Memphis, TN, 1954. (Bowers)

"British Charter of Liberties and Privileges 1683," revised 1691. New York Colonial Charter,   (BCLP)

Doherty, Frank J. *"Settlers of Beekman Patent, "* 1990, (Doherty)

Fernow's, *New York in the Revolution*, (NYIR)

Grun, Bernard, *The Timetables of History*, Published by, Simon & Schuster, NY, NY, Third Revised Edition, 1991. (Grun)

Historical Association of South Jefferson County, *The War of 1812*, Pub. Web (HASJC)

Jewell, Roger L., *The Sawmill River Valley War*, Jewell Histories, Fairfield, PA, 2009. (Jewell)

Morison, Samuel Eliot, & Commager, Henry, Steele, *The Growth of the American Republic, Vol 1*, Oxford University Press, New York, NY, 1962. (Morison)

Muller, Charles, T*he Darkest Day – 1814*, Modern Literary Editions Publishing Company, NY, NY, 1963. (Muller)

Old Dutch Church Record, Book One, Sleepy Hollow, (ODCR)

Perkins, Bradford, *The Causes of the War of 1812*, University of Michigan, Holt, Rinehart and Winston, NY, NY, 1962. (Perkins)

Rensselear, Steven, "*Rensselearwyck Manor Papers*," SC7079, Index to leases A-L, Richard Jewell leased a farm in Rensselearville, lot 314, 164 ½ acres, April 12, 1794. (RMP)

Saratogian, The, *History of Saratoga New York*, the Boston History Company, Publishers 1899.

Scott, Winfield, *Lieut. General, LLD, Memoirs, Vol. One*, New York, 1864, (Scott)

Stoke, Elliott G., *History of Cayuga County*, (About 1878) (Old book on line scanned in) (Stoke)

Sylvester, Nathaniel Bartlett, *History of Saratoga County*, New York, 1878
(Mostly from Web.) (Sylvester)

Thwaites, Reuben, *Collections of the State Historical Society of Wisconsin*, Vol. XI, Madison, Wisconsin, State Printers, 1888. (New York Feudal Problem) (Wisc. SHS 11)

Tompkins, Daniel, *"Governor D. Tompkins Papers"* From Web, E-Book No. one, (Tompkins)

Waller, George, *Sartatoga – Saga of an Impious Era*, Bonanza Books, New York, 1966 (Waller)

Wilder, Patrick A., *"The Battle of Sackett's Harbor - 1813"*, The Nautical & Aviation Publishing Company of America
(Wilder)

National Archives Source:

Revolutionary War & War of 1812

George Jewell papers - No. R 5585 – New York, Transcribed by Author, March 11,   2008.   Abv. (RW-R5585)

1812- Pension Applications, Collected 7/27/2011, by Author, from original documents

James George Jewell – Applicant wife Betsey –. – Certificate no WC- 16431

(Capt Jacob Arnold's & Captain Josiah Perry's Company of NY Militia as a private)

Abv. (PA-WC16431).

George Jewell & Mary, his Wife Applicant – Certificate no. (WF – 11938)
(Served as a private in the 13 Infantry of the US Regulars)

Abv. (PA-WF11938)

Jewel Family Records: (JFR)

Wills: Abv. (JFR-W)

Elizabeth (Lizzy) Jewel's Will – Westchester County Archives
George Jewel's Will, 1765 (same)
John Jewel's Will, (? 1835?) (same)
William Jewel's, Death Inventory, 1808, County Records
Ketchum's Will. (Loom) (Will Abstract of Nathaniel Ketchum, 9 Sep 1738, Wilton Parish, Norwalk Twp., Fairfield Co., Conn. Colony: Original will at Wilton Public Library
Wills Buckhout, *Settlers of Beekman Patent Vol. 3,* 1993, p – 934

Deeds: Abv. (JFR-D)

> Joseph H. Jewell, Sale deed, 1846.
> Thomas Jewell, Sale Deed, 1846.
> States Jewel's, Purchas of his son's Property.
> States & his Brother William Purchas of property by
> Lake Saratoga

Web Sites:

Historical Association of South Jefferson County, *The War of 1812,* Pub. Web (HASJC)

"New York In The Revolution As Colony And State" Vol. I. "A Compilation of Documents and Records from the Office of State Comptroller, Albany, N. Y., J. B. Lyon Co, Printers 1904, Transcribed by Coralynn Brown, 1812 Sackett's Harbor File, (Book that tell the positions at the Battle Saratoga) (ch-4) (NYIR)

End notes:

[1] History Book
[2] Sylvester, Jewell p - 229
[3] Sylvester, Congress Spr. P - 229
[4] Nat Arc NOR558
[5] Nat Arc NOR558
[6] Jewell p - 227
[7] Waller p - 153
[8] JFR Will Elizabeth
[9] Sylvester p - 221
[10] JFR Will, William
[11] JFR Bible, Asa
[12] Afloat & Ashore, Ch30
[13] Sloops of the Hudson
[14] JFR Family Tree
[15] Sylvester, p- ? Jenny Mc Cree
[16] JFR Will, Elizabeth
[17] Jewell Bridge Research
[18] Sylvester p - ? Toll's Mill
[19] JFR Wills, William
[20] Jewell's Corner Map
[21] JFR Deeds, Tom's
[22] Sylvester, p - Lot 27 &28 dev, Jewell Bridge
[23] Jewell p - 142
[24] Jewell, p – 17, location of home farm
[25] History
[26] History, Peace Treaty 1782
[27] Rensselear Will, Web.
[28] SHCR, p 74,
[29] NYIR, p -
[30] Sleepy Hollow Cemetery, visited graves
[31] JFR Wills, William's
[32] ODCR, Birth Records, Jewel Children
[33] Jewell, Cover Sketch
[34] NYIR, p - Dutchess County History
[35] NYIR, p -/ Dutchess County History

[36] Book, Battle of Saratoga ?
[37] Waller, P - 68
[38] JFR Wills, Ketchum
[39] JFR, Bible, Asa
[40] Doherty, Vol. 3, p – 934, Will of John Buckhout
[41] History, NY Colonial Charter, Web
[42] History, US Constitutional Convention 1787&1788
[43] Web Governor Clinton was against the US Constitution
[44] NYIR, NY Paid off debts
[45] Web, New York Patent Histories
[46] Rent Wars, "Free holders" voting controls
[47] Bayard, p – 143, 144
[48] JFR Deeds, George
[49] Sylvester, web Batchellerville Bridge
[50] JFR Deed, Joseph's
[51] Sylvester, p – 223 Three Jewell boys moved to Lake Saratoga
[52] Jefferson, Note on Public Schools
[53] Jewell, p – 210
[54] Sylvester, p - ___ Reminiscence of Mr. St. John's
[55] JFR Deed, Thomas
[56] History, web: Napoleon war started , 1803
[57] Web: Burr & Hamilton Duel, Americas Library.gov
[58] Bayard, p -143,144, Hamilton's land policy
[59] Rosenburg, p - 45
[60] Web: rent Wars, Incomplete Sales
[61] Nat Arc, RW - No R558, local History
[62] Rosenburg, p - 6
[63] Waller, p – 68, Map of Saratoga County
[64] Perkins, p – 32&34. Quote
[65] Thompkins, Web: E-book No. 1, The embargo Act of 1807
[66] JFR Will, William , Local county records
[67] Web: Wikipedia, Embargo act of 1870
[68] Nat Arc, PA – WC - 16431
[69] Tompkins, p - 48, Albany 13th August, 1812 Order
[70] Web: War of 1812, Battle of Queenston Heights
[71] Nat Arc, PA NO WC 16431; PA WF - 11938
[72] Tompkins, James orders, Book one, p 438 - 439
[73] Battle of Queenston Heights, Scott, p - 62
[74] Sylvester, p - ___

[75] HASJC, Defense of Sackett's Harbor

[76] HASJC, The Ship Pike then on the stocks

[77] HASJC, Fort Tompkins , 200 dismounted dragoons

[78] HASJC, "They found something to fire at."

[79] Wilder p – 97, map

[80] Wilder p – 87, "a fire of musketry from the Island" "By now most of the Volunteers had left the island"

[81] Wilder p – 88, "As ordered, the Volunteers joined Brown on the mainland and positioned themselves directly across the causeway

[82] Wilder p – 89, Mills Albany Volunteers held their fire until the advancing enemy was within 60 paces.

[83] Wilder p – 101, Beresford's fire going over fort Tompkins and caused confusion for the sailors.

[84] Web: The United States Army in the War of 1812, p-223. Lt Col John Christie's Letter 10/13/1812.

[85] PA-WF 11938, children's names

[86]PA- WC - 16431 "On the return home Jewel along with a number of others armed and equipped enlisted under Captain Joseph Welch and went to Niagara being gone 3 months more"

[87] Web: Wikipedia, War of 1812, the burning of Newark

[88] Thompkins, Web: e-book, Letters of William b. Rodchester on the fall of Niagara.

[89] Rochester Letters, no of men

[90] Fall of Niagara, number in fort

[91] Web: Parks of Canada, War of 1812, capture of fort Niagara

[92] Web: Map ref ??

[93] Hall's Report, Register of state papers, Vol. one, p - 380

[94] Hall's Report, Register of State papers, Vol one, p - 380

[95] PA- WC - 16431

[96] Web: Burning of Buffolo

[97] Week's Letter, Army Heritage center files

[98] Web: War and Security, The Fall of Paris 30-31 March, 1814, Napoleon's Abdication.

[99] PA –WC - 16431

[100] PA-WC-16431 & Grun

[101] PA WC-16431

[102] Web: Christy's report on the 13th

[103] Web: Christy's Report on the 13th

[104] PA-WF11938, George's Death date

[105] JFR Deed, Joseph's deed, 1846
[106] Web: Wikipedia, Year without a summer
[107] Web:, Wikipedia, , Lord Byron's poem, "Darkness"
[108] JFR Deed, Toll's Deed, Sale of mill
[109] Web: Wikipedia, Year without a summer

[110] JFR Family tree, Abe's death
[111] JFR, family tree, PA –WC- 16431
[112] Web: Wikipedia, Second bank of the United States
[113] Web: revised New York constitution 1821
[114] Web: land grant acerages
[115] Schlesinger, p – 45, Quote
[116] Schlesinger, p – 72, Quote, Andrew Jackson, The Age of Jackson
[117] Schlesinger, p – 70, quote, (same as above)
[118] Rensselearwick papers, Quote rent wars
[119] Rensselearwick Papers, Quote rent wars
[120] JFR Deeds, Thomas and Joseph's
[121] Local History

www.ingramcontent.com/pod-product-compliance
Lightning Source LLC
Chambersburg PA
CBHW052006090426
42741CB00008B/1576